Reflections by the Lake

Reflections by the Lake

Journaling Life's Journey

JANICE GRAY KOLB

Blue Dolphin Publishing

Published by Blue Dolphin Publishing, Inc.
P.O. Box 8, Nevada City, CA 95959
Orders: 1-800-643-0765
Web: www.bluedolphinpublishing.com

ISBN: 978-1-57733-245-9

Library of Congress Cataloging-in-Publication Data

Kolb, Janice E. M.
   Reflections by the lake : journaling life's journey / Janice Gray Kolb.
      p. cm.
   ISBN 978-1-57733-245-9 (pbk. : alk. paper)
   1. Kolb, Janice E. M.—Diaries. 2. Diaries—Authorship—Religious aspects.
3. Human-animal relationships—Religious aspects. 4. Spiritual life.
5. Meditations. I. Title.
   BL73.K65A3 2010
   204.092—dc22
   [B]
                                                    2010019772

A portion of any profits realized by sales of this book will be used to support
various animal charities.

Photos by the author.

Cover photo is the view from the author's writing room: one of our gardens by
the lake. The statue of the angel reading a book (perhaps a journal) is a gift
from Dennis and Patti Clancy.

Printed in the United States of America

5   4   3   2   1

*Dedicated
to my
beloved feline
soulmate
Rochester*

and

*to my
beloved
husband and soulmate
Bob*

and

*to Rochester's and my
spiritual friend
Chris Comins
who is a blessing and strength
on this continuing Journey.*

We wish to acknowledge the passing of
a dearly loved animal companion.
A member of the VanDorick family—
daughter Janna and son-in-law Bill, Dahlia, Cole and Rebecca—
but very dear to us as well.

HONEY
entered Heaven
February 19, 2010

In luxury of remembrance and with eternal love and gratefulness
I remember
Daniel T. Deane
faithful friend and heart encourager
who loved his God and cared about animals deeply.
He entered Heaven
March 16, 2010
HE WILL BE SADLY MISSED

Contents

A Word in Preparation

ONE OF THE CONSTANTS IN THE AUTHOR'S LIFE has been the need to keep a journal. For her the journal serves a variety of purposes. It not only records events and experiences and focuses on issues currently active in her life, but analyzes them. It also explores thought processes the writer is experiencing, and provides a reference point for future thoughts. In my opinion a journal and a diary are two different things. While a diary is a simple recording of thoughts and events, a journal also involves study and analysis of the writers life and the direction that life is taking. It provides reflections and observations that are written down so that when the writer returns she can examine and interpret her experiences and observations in order to better understand them. The journal becomes a check-list for her life's goals and enables those goals for her life to be fulfilled to a greater degree. In reviewing what was previously written the author may develop a much clearer view of the events that were recorded. She may then be in a better position to analyze what her real goal was, what really happened, was her response correct, and how could she have done better. She may also be in a better position to determine the significance of the recorded event and reflect on what she learned, what new insights were gained and how she now feels about that situation.

The author has taken five of the many dozens of journals she has written over a lifetime, and replicated some of the jottings there exactly as they appeared. No effort was made to correct grammar or sentence structure, or even to put her thoughts in a more readable form. They appear in this book exactly as she wrote them even though at the time she may have been tired or sad, or upset or exuberant. The only alterations I am aware of are some deletions made because of their personal nature or the effect they may have on the person involved reading them in this book. The journals were in many ways tools of self-help. Sometimes, when faced with confounding issues, it seems necessary to find a shoulder to lean on, or an ear that is sympathetic, or a place to pour your soul into when advice is not the needed entity, but a silent and attentive listener is.

To expose yourself to possible humiliation by revealing things from those secret places in your mind can present a real challenge. She has done that here in an attempt to help others as she has helped herself. Writing a journal has absolutely and surely helped her. Generally speaking, many fears have departed and others have been lessened. She has provided much to her own happiness by simply recording events and reactions, then later reading and reviewing them. As she has been helped by reading many journals written by others, she now adds to this list parts of her journals so that help can be shared.

Because her life has been built around an active meditation and prayer life, she has separated the chapters involving journal entries with chapters on various aspects of meditation. These meditations contain poems, quotations, and real helps for allowing you to find peace and contentment.

The passing of her beloved cat companion and friend Rochester has had a profound effect on her life. By confronting his loss, she has been able to change much in her life. Her reading habits have changed dramatically since his passing. Her entire reading now seems focused on the afterlife genre. As a result her attention is now directed toward life, and concerns about death have been eliminated. The awesome reality of death holds no fears for her. Many of life's doubts have been replaced by absolute certainties and she is a happier person. As a result of reading, meditation, and reviewing her own journal entries, she is better qualified to face life's every day assaults that would previously have negatively impacted her.

By reading this book it is the authors wish and expectation that some of the truths that she has discovered will be imparted to you, and that you will find thoughts of real value that you will appropriate to enhance and fulfill your own life.

Robert A. Kolb Jr.

Acknowledgments

May the words of this book—and the meditation of our hearts
(the readers—and mine)—give glory to God
all glory to my Christ
and love and gratitude to Blessed Mother Mary
who always intercedes.

I wish to thank my
Guardian Angel
and my special Angels
who are ever present.

I wish to express my deepest appreciation to Paul M. Clemens,
publisher of Blue Dolphin Publishing, for believing in this book and for
his kindness and grief support and to all his capable staff who helped in
so many ways. I especially thank Linda Maxwell, Diane Winslow, and
Barb Brumbelow for their fine work and their friendship.

I wish to thank Rochester for his constant love, presence, devotion,
inspiration, and teachings throughout our life together. Because of him
this book was written.

I am deeply grateful to my husband Bob for his love and support,
for believing in me, and for our life together in New Hampshire.
I am grateful too for the time he gave
in endless hours typing this manuscript.

I wish to thank
St. Francis of Assisi
and
St. Martin dePorres
for their great love and protection of all God's creatures.

Introduction

*"To enter the world of real magic,
you must enter the dimension of spirituality."*
—Dr. Wayne W. Dyer from *Staying on the Path*

THE WRITINGS IN THIS BOOK are extremely personal and that is why I have decided to share them with you. Because they are writings that helped me along my way, I feel they might also help others. I have written several previous books in journal form and too written about the subject of journal keeping in a portion of each of my books, but I have never done what I am doing now.

In this book I am allowing writings from five of my journals to be read by you, and many writings also from a journal notebook. The latter writings in the soft back 8x10 notebook are mainly concerning the meditative state and dream state and Hypnogogic Imagery.

The other four journals are copied out directly just for you from my own 6x9-inch hard back journals with lovely covers. There is a separate one that does not have specific entries shared, but in general speaks about the subject matter of my fourth published book titled *Journal of Love: Spiritual Communication with Animals Through Journal Writing*. I believe you will find this very unusual and delightful—and if you have never been exposed to such experiences, beliefs, exchanges and possibilities, it may be very enlightening and life changing. There are many, many more persons out there in this world (and some may truly think I AM "out there.") than just myself with similar encounters and beliefs, and many other books have been written on such subject matter similar to mine that have inspired me.

These journals I share here with you now contain writings from my heart and soul written in privacy when I have desperately needed to write in order to help myself, or to make entries when I was in my rather constant state of bliss here in the woods by the lake, or to discuss in my journals the books I was writing or have written and to record things in them pertaining to these books. Some family matters are throughout but mainly these journals were kept to accompany me and to confide in while I wrote my books. Unless there is something written too personal that involves someone other than myself, the journals are left intact. I will not embarrass anyone for the sake of keeping a journal totally "as is" for this book.

To reveal private journals never meant for other eyes but your own can be daunting, embarrassing, demeaning and frightening. It requires much prayer. But I have been helped in the past and the present by others, men, women, teenagers and children, who have done similar, and if I am ridiculed or thought extremely odd or strange it does not matter to me now. The fear is gone. I trod a higher path and for a precious cause—for if this book can help even one other person in a way or ways I will never know or in the same or similar ways I have been helped by others revealing their minds and souls, then it will be worth my being led to share my personal thoughts and angst.

Some years ago, after the completion of my writing of *The Enchantment of Writing: Spiritual Healing and Delight Through the Written Word*, my publisher Paul Clemens asked if I would ever consider revealing some of my personal journals in order to instill the desire in young people to acquire the incentive to write in their own journals. I thought that was a wonderful idea but at that time I was a bit anxious about doing such a thing for a number of personal reasons. My life and its circumstances and problems were not the same then as they are now. I am a different person now, a stronger one, and I live in a different dimension and totally in the moment, and I have been shown things and experienced them and I will never be as I was before. I have spoken of this in my books written since 2002. I do not mean I was a bad person before. I most certainly hope not ever! I always tried my best and followed a path of spirituality. But the passing of my beloved little companion Rochester in 2002 changed my life, just as he changed it when he entered it in 1986. An animal companion in life can also be a spiritual teacher to enlightenment and all I did was enhanced, my spiritual life, writing, living, and my meditative practices, by my connection to and great love for Rochester and his mutual love for me both in his life time on earth and after passing to eternal time. And his constant companionship both then and now. He has truly been a spiritual guide sent by God and many can deeply understand that and many cannot. Therefore, to share my personal journals now I can do, whereas I could not do so before March 2002.

Jean Houston writes in her amazing book that I have read multiple times and dip back into time and time again titled *Mystical Dogs: Animals as Guides to Our Inner Life.*

> *Animals seem to live in another domain of time and space, one that transcends our clocks and mappings. Maybe because they do not read the maps they can find us across thousands of miles and in spite of impossible odds.*

She goes on to say how they seem to pick up on the broadcast beam of their beloved humans and some of our reverence before animals is that they seem to belong to some eternal time beyond time. Yes, I am living that with Rochester. She states: "Each animal that we have known is in some way, not dead even though we may have attended their dying." And so it is with Rochester.

I am a new and different and stronger person and because of that I can reveal even more of my mind and heart and life, and hopefully this can help others as I have been helped by those who also do so. It does not mean I have left out things in these journals for the reader to read that might make me seem less. I have not. I was what I was then and I am what I am now and if even one sentence or passage can help someone or lead them to write also, that is what I desire. These journals are for any age, not intended for young or old, just anyone. I hope they will inspire writing as was originally intended when I was asked some years ago to reveal some of my journals. I present them now to you.

Before closing these thoughts and confessions I share some words with you that I have included in similar ways in most of my previous Introductions in my books. Perhaps they will help you to come to know me in a deeper and clearer sense.

As I have written in each of my previous books—

As you read this book, know a little creature of God is present. Rochester has been completely with me in the pages of eleven of my twelve previous books and has been with me in this one. Before he was born I co-authored a book with Bob—but the eleven that followed I co-authored with Rochester. Rochester has remained with me in spirit since his passing though he is also in Heaven. This book and any other I have written only came into being because his "Angel Being" came into my life. You will sense his presence. His love and spiritual presence are inspiring me and we communicate deeply. His paw prints are on each page. He is all love, a precious soul, and I pay tribute to him now and always. He is my Angel.

Since my journals (and steno pads) are the places in which I write my original and deepest thoughts and my poems, some poems in this book of journals have appeared in a number of my previous books.

And now to our journey along the way as we travel this corridor to Eternity. Perhaps you will bring your own journal as well as mine for the journey. Yes, I think you may be inspired to write.

God Bless You!

Janice Gray Kolb
East Wakefield, New Hampshire

THE PILGRIM

Who can say whom God will send
To be your Angel, guide and friend.
Angels come in many forms
To be with you in all life's storms.
And we should not assume and say
A winged Angel shows the way.

Very early on I found
My Angel does not make a sound.
He speaks no words that you will hear
His messages are for my ear.
He guides me gently to the light
On dear soft marshmallow paws of white.
And on that passage I now trod
He leads me on to meet my God.

With great love   Jan
for my Angel   April 8, 2005
Rochester—

The Importance and Holiness of Journal Keeping

"There are about thirty of them now—notebooks of different sizes,
every page of them filled up with handwriting.
I hardly ever read them, but I've got one open now."
—Thomas Mallon, *A Book of One's Own:*
People and Their Diaries

MANY ARE CONFUSED AS TO WHAT TO CALL THEM—a diary or a journal. After years of writing in them and reading many, many books about them and personal ones written and published by others, I believe they are basically the same. Author and diarist Thomas Mallon also believes this and in fact states that the two terms are hopelessly muddled and both are rooted in the idea of dailyness. It really does not matter what you call them as long as you write. As time passes I have come to know that. You can use the term diary or journal.

However in my earlier book *Higher Ground* (and I cannot argue with these thoughts either for I was once a young girl as is written about) I wrote that a journal is not a day by day diary as we often remember a diary from our childhood with limited lines and lock and key and meant for brief entries of weather or comments about boyfriends or proms or one's school work. A journal is so much more and used in complete freedom and meant for total expression and many pages can be used at one writing and not merely one small lined page or space. You create your journal. It is conceived in your spirit and born as a living extension of yourself emotionally, psychologically and spiritually. My book *Higher Ground* was written from a journal that I kept when I came to our cottage in the woods in 1986 and made a retreat for a week with only my kitten Rochester as my companion. I had never stayed in the woods before without Bob and my children. I have tried since I was a child to daily write in a diary (or journal) and at times succeeded. And some had locks and keys. But more often great lapses would occur in my journals. To one who writes in this form it can be very upsetting at times—other times it can be handled well and one just continues. But basically always that particular lapse where one may not have written for several days or weeks or months is plaguing the writer until he moves on and keeps writing and convinces himself it is impossible to remember all the segments of time in detail he let lapse, and continuing rather proves himself to himself,—and says, "See, you are not so bad after all." I am speaking for myself in that last sentence for I carry guilt continually within me, so an empty page or more may hit me harder than it does most, but I suspect the majority of serious journal keepers are much like myself. Forgive me if that is not so. I just have my suspicions from published journals of others that I have read or from authors writing about journal keeping but that have not published their own.

I do not want to give the impression that keeping a journal is unpleasant and filled with rules. It is not! It is quite the opposite! It is wonderful! There are no rules! That is the beauty of it all. I would not have been writing in journals for all of these years if it were not so.

For the past thirty years or more it has been my custom to actually make the sign of the cross with my pen on the top of each piece of paper I write on in a letter, in a journal, brief notes, or on anything I write. It is making a blessing on my words and on the recipient if it is a letter, and is a reminder of God's presence. It is just a practice I was led by the spirit to do. There are crosses in pencil on every sheet of loose leaf paper I have filled as I write this present manuscript now. I feel that Jesus was showing me that our writing is Holy and should be respected. A cross is at the top of every handwritten page of every manuscript I have ever written. My journals, from sometime in the seventies on, all have crosses on every page. You may wish to pray and be open to a similar way to remind yourself that your writing is spiritual and Holy, for it is. Then you will respect it as a Holy discipline and practice.

Some years after I began doing this I read in a journal of Thomas Merton's, a well known Monk who had lived in the Abbey of Gethsemane in Kentucky, that he too inscribed a cross at the top of all his written pages. He too kept journals and wrote books and is known far and wide by people of all faiths and especially by his journal *Sign of Jonas*. He was a kindred spirit whom I came to know through his many books. His writings caused a deep desire to keep writing in my journals and to enter the Catholic Church. He too had been a convert, a Protestant as I was and will always be in my heart, along with being a Catholic. I was already Monk-like in my prayer life and need for solitude. His journals fed my soul.

Above all, I made the sign of the cross on Rochester's forehead every single night of his life with me before we went to sleep and I still do in spirit.

If we come into a new awareness and realize that this is the only moment we have like this or ever shall have, then we are more apt to capture some of those moments in writing. I have said elsewhere in this book that I live in the present moment. Time is no longer as it once was to me before 2002. When a person writes there is an extraordinary relationship between mind and heart, and in the hand as it writes. What happens to us while writing is far more important than what is written. Some hidden capacity seems to emerge and we sense subtle changes in us and things seem to be growing within and we feel the need to keep writing. It is as if a veil lifts. Writing does that! In my book *Beside the Still Waters: Creative Meditations from the Woods* I relate in my meditation of Journal Keeping that one spiritual writer's thoughts I recorded years ago in my journal for he compared journal writing to the experience of Emmaus, "Did not our hearts burn within us as He talked to us and explained the scripture to us" (Luke 24:32). Since I owned an artist's framed interpretation of the scripture "The Road to Emmaus" and bought it because the scripture touched my soul, this writer's comparison also spoke to me. It was a beautiful comparison!

If we take time to write in our journal we discover that writing is a path into what is going on and developing within ourselves. Without writing we may never discover all that is within because the more we write the more surfaces and is revealed. It just happens. Writing can be a powerful way of prayer and a key to dialogue and self-understanding. Writing stimulates the inner process. It has that power and causes us to go further inward. Expressing oneself in words opens the floodgates if we just keep our hand moving. We will write things that are beyond comprehension to us because we will be drawn into an understanding of our very own existence. If we each write regularly, no matter how briefly, we will find the desire to write more and more. And more will be revealed and surface during our writing. We capture things that are deeper than our consciousness.

Before I share a quotation of great meaning to me for years by Thomas Merton, I would like to share a special happening. I have written in several books of my obstetrician friend Dr. Francis McGeary who also was Monk-like and appreciated Thomas Merton. I called my friend "Friar Francis." My book *Higher Ground* helped him greatly in regard to our mutual problem of "Irregular People," and he sent a copy of it to the Trappist Monastery where Thomas Merton had lived and where he himself had once made a retreat. He received from a monk a beautiful and affirming reply concerning *Higher Ground* and that he and others had read it. This touched me so deeply and gave me hope that it would help others (and it has!) for Friar Francis sent it to the monastery of Gethsemane in manuscript form before it was published. Francis passed away and went to Heaven before my book came into the world.

There should be at least one room, or some corner, where no one will find you and disturb you or notice you. You should be able to untether yourself from the world and set yourself free, loosing all the fine strings and strands of tension that bind you by sight, by sound, by thought, to the presence of other men."

—Thomas Merton, *New Seeds of Contemplation*

This quotation describes my writing/prayer room in the front of the cottage overlooking the lake. Rochester still daily shares it with me in spirit. We always write and pray here together. But though it is best to have a quiet room or corner to be in when you write in your journal, please do not not write if there is not a special place. Just write in whatever space you consider all yours. It can be anywhere including a chair somewhere in your home, a corner of your yard in nice weather, in your car, or on the porch. It will call to you once you stand with journal and pen in hand. The Angels will know your wonderful intention and will have found you your special place. Just go!

WRITING THERAPY

My writing is a deepening need
And pen slips o'er the page with speed.
And oft when I look back to read—
I see God meant my soul to feed!

But when my hand goes on a spree—
It is no certain guarantee—
That it brings inward harmony,
Sometimes it stirs up dark debris!

And then I must stop to inspect—
And interject—pause and reflect—
And disconnect with all neglect—
In retrospect—pray and correct!

And now my pen glides on with ease-
My thoughts are cleansed and I am pleased—
For I have dealt with all disease
Entrapped in those soliloquies!

If I'm to live—then I must write!
It brings delight—and new insight!
It lessens fright—makes my soul bright—
If every night—I can "moonlight."

In silent times—then things external
Are blotted out—and the Eternal—
Touches me—and with my journal,
I write and live—in hours nocturnal!

Dedicated to   Jan
Writing

As a little spiritual nudge to begin your own journal writing, I share with you now my journal from March 13, 2000 to July 5, 2000. You have no idea how awkward I feel—and yet if it can inspire anyone else to write and be helped, then so be it.

All Things Are Possible

*T*HIS JOURNAL IS MEANT TO SERVE as an inspirational format for personal growth, revelation and development
BEGUN MARCH 13, 2000 — COMPLETED JULY 5, 2000

This 5x8 journal is the lovely color purple in a horizontal washboard-type dimensionally ridged cover. A rectangular 3.5x5 other-worldly picture is an inset in the purple cover. It is of three enchanting soft pale green frogs with large dark eyes looking at me and purple iris and green leaves and a spotted pale green dragonfly amongst them. My favorite colors—green and purple. The frogs are on a purple and gold symbolic large line ring within the flowers.

This journal was given to me by my friend (Rev.) Don Richards—and in the inscription within he includes he found it in Juneau, Alaska. He closes with the words:

May your words carry wisdom and power

Christmas 1999

On this same page is another printed inscription with a rune symbol—a part of the journal.

You are your life's author.
Let the words written here
by your own hand
be your inspiration.

At the top of all the pages in pale ink is printed upon a pale rune symbol:

> *There is power*
> *in your vision*
> *and wisdom*
> *in you words*

On the alternate pages it states:

> *Believe — Imagine — Dream*

Ask a toad what is beauty?... a female with two great round eyes coming out of her little head, large flat mouth, a yellow belly and a brown back.

—Voltaire

HIGHER GROUND
MARCH 13, 2000

Frog

The frog has been associated with regeneration and change since ancient time, doubtless because of its extraordinary metamorphosis from egg to tadpole to four legged creature. Not surprisingly, it is also associated with magic

—Peg Streep, *Altars Made Easy*

Images of frogs can be used on an altar and elsewhere to symbolize transformation. Their appearances in various forms are important to me here on Higher Ground and their voices. From the tiny peepers that we cannot see but that break forth in singing in early spring every night at dusk, to the various others that do make regular appearances—I say welcome.

> *Writing is the best instruction.*
> *Let your pen teach you.*
> *Ask hard questions.*
> *Discover answers with*
> *your pen and a little quiet.*

—MaryAnne Radmacher-Hershey

When you find the courage to change at mid-life, a miracle happens. Your character is opened, deepened, strengthened and softened. You return to your soul's highest values and are prepared to create your legacy; and imprint of your dream for our world—a dream that came true in the second half of life.

—Angeles Arrien, Ph.D.

I did this—and am still in the process. Maybe I am the only one who realizes this. I am the only one.

Those who are without compassion cannot see what is seen with the eyes of compassion.

—Thich Nhat Hanh, *The Miracle of Mindfulness:
A Manual on Meditation*

Write it in your heart that every day is the best day in the year.

—Unknown

MARCH 18, 2000

My beloved little Rochester. I place his picture in here and our book cover (it is a picture of the cover of our book *Compassion for All Creatures* which has his precious picture on the cover, so I can meditate on him as I write or at any time). He looks out at me in such love and I look deep into his eyes. We are one. When I see this picture of him staring out at me from the shelves at Bookland it often makes me cry. And always I stand still before him and tell him my love. That this picture of him is all over the United States, in many European countries, Australia and the Internet—touches my heart and soul. He is meant to touch the world.

SUNDAY, MARCH 19, 2000

*Standing quietly by the fence,
you smile your wondrous smile.
I am speechless, and my senses filled
by the sounds of your beautiful song.*

This poem goes on to say that the song is both beginingless and endless and that he bows deeply to the flower. It was written by a friend of Thich Nhat Hanh's who died as a young man over thirty years ago. Thich Nhat Hanh writes about it and asks, "Do you see?" He goes on to tell us that the curtain was drawn back for only a second, and the poet could see.

He tells us further that the Dahlia is so commonplace that most people do not truly see it. Then he shares that if you can hear its eternal song and see its miraculous smile, then it is no longer an ordinary flower. He also writes that after his friend died, people found many beautiful poems he had written, and Thich was startled when he read this poem. He thinks it is very beautiful yet has only a few short lines. It is very beautiful to me too. The poet passed by the fence and saw the little flower and saw it very deeply and, struck by the sight of it, he stopped and wrote the poem. I appreciate this so much. Poems mean very much to me. Thich also writes that he enjoys the poem very much and goes on to say that you might think the poet was a mystic because his way of looking at it and seeing things is very deep, but he was just an ordinary person.

He goes on to say that he does not know how or why the poet was able to see as he did, but it is exactly the way we practice mindfulness.

He tells me that to be in touch with life I should look deeply as I drink tea, walk, sit down or arrange flowers. He tells me too that the secret of success is that I am really myself, and when I am really myself, I can then encounter life in the present moment. I will share the poem and comments with Janna and Dahlia.

THURSDAY, APRIL 6, 2000

I have not done a good job of writing in here. For that I am sorry. It was a year ago tomorrow that I gave my hour's talk at the Unicorn Books and Spiritual Resource Center in Arlington, Massachusetts.

That was a wonderful experience and I cannot believe it has been a year. I was amazed at myself because I thought I would be so frightened beforehand and while doing it. No matter how I tried to prepare for it, I could not. I was so relaxed. Finally right near the date, days before, I forced myself to write what I wanted to include briefly on index cards. I went over them only about twice. And the night I gave the talk I barely used them, in fact when I glanced at them they sort of made me lose my train of thought. Then twilight came and there was not much light in the second-floor room of the bookstore to even read the cards by, so I did the entire talk so freely and from my heart. Everyone seemed to enjoy it too. Everyone was so nice and all the rows of chairs were filled and I felt at ease. I wore my nice black two piece dress I wore to George's and Val's wedding. When I had just finished (and there was also a question and answer period too), George and Val and Jameson walked in. It was so sweet of them to come. But they had gotten lost coming from Rhode Island and did not arrive until it was all over. But it meant a lot to me, and Bob was very supportive beforehand and that night. And the Clancys, Joanne and Terry too, were all so kind and said how much they enjoyed it as did Verna who works at the store and asked me to give the talk. But all the people seemed to like it. It was a good experience for me and gave me confidence. I know Rochester was at home praying for me. Bob and I went out to dinner beforehand even at Boston Market and it was so delicious and I could not believe how relaxed I was before giving the talk.

Afterwards Joanne invited us back to her house and that was so nice and we talked for a long time at her kitchen table and she ordered pizza for us all and we ate together. It was all so unwinding and relaxing. She is very loving and we always enjoy talking. For several years I have exclusively been using a lovely coffee mug that is shades of lavender and green—my favorite colors, and it turned out that the cup belonged to a set of Joanne's and somehow had gotten up here in New Hampshire to Dennis's cottage. He knew it was here and was sweet and said to keep it. I never use another mug. When Joanne came to give Bob and me each a Reiki session two or three years ago she saw the cup I was raving about when we had tea and told me it was hers and she was thrilled I had it. She had a whole set of them! She was so sweet. Well, this night after my talk when we went back to her house she served me in a matching mug to the one I love and use here and insisted I take it home. So I have two of them now I alternate with and have tea in one now here as I am writing. I just wanted to record all these things about that night I gave the talk even though I am certain I did record them a year ago. I am grateful to have had the experience.

In Hypnogogic Imagery in meditation I saw clearly amazing things. I saw Bob just sitting looking at me, and Rochester standing on the living room stairs looking at me as I sat on the sofa as I do at night. I was meditating in my chair in my writing room before writing. The other image I saw so clearly was that of three large piliated woodpeckers all surrounding one of the birch trees out front of my window. They were on the same birch. It was so real. Last week Bob and I spotted a piliated woodpecker for the first time in about eight years! They are rare. He was in a pine tree by my prayer chair and had Bob not looked out at that minute we would have missed him. Bob quickly told me and we both saw him on the branch—and then he took off and his wing span was enormous! He flew out over the lake. We were thrilled to see him. The Hairy and Downy woodpeckers come constantly year round to our suet feeder. It is interesting I saw the real piliated woodpecker last week, then three in hynogogic imagery this week. Perhaps the original was in my subconscious and came through this week in the other way. It is all a mystery that these images can be seen so clearly on the inner eye.

The last two days I have spent writing a chapter for my new book on the Peepers. I like what I have written. It is appropriate. I am reporting about it here in my frog journal too.

FRIDAY, APRIL 7, 2000

We had a nice day today in Sanford and now are relaxing. I will only write a few lines. It was the first time in years I could not go to Bookland. As I approached the store I felt such sadness. A sign on the door said it was closed and to visit the other Bookland stores in Saco and I forget where else.

I stood with my face pressed against the glass and looked in. The entire store was empty of every shelf. The only thing remaining was the central raised booth area where you checked out with the sweet people that worked there, like Cheryl and Rob and others. It was so huge inside when empty, and so stark and naked and I cried. I could not help it. It just broke me up. I have cried each time I walked out of it the last three times since learning it would close. Today was the bleakest to see it this way. It was such a joy in my life. I am so thankful I met Cheryl and Rob there and had so many lovely experiences regarding my own books. But I am thankful for the few years I had too before my own books were in the store. I am thankful for each hour spent there, and I never spent less than an hour and usually more. I am thankful for the browsing, the books there, and all the books I now own that I bought there through the years. It is really a deep loss to me that it has closed—like a death.

On the way into Sanford I stopped for only the second time and went into the Upper Story Bookshop that is on the right of Main Street before the library shortly after on the left. The first time I was in that store was several years ago out of curiosity but that was all. Father Edmund bought my *Compassion for All Creatures* in that store but they did not have any today. It is a lovely store with many small rooms but all the books on all the shelves floor to ceiling face front, so they really do not have many books. There may be only five or six books per shelf and all shelves were not filled. They sell other things too; postcards, stationery, tee shirts, greeting cards, jewelry. It is a sweet store but does not have nearly the volume of books that Bookland had. There is an upper story I did not go up, but a little boy and his mother did. I thought maybe children's books were up there. I bought three books, one from outside on a bookcase where sale books were and originally $8.95, but $2.95 today. It is by Melody Beattie and I have other books by her that I like and reread. This is called *A Reason to Live,* concerning suicide. Then full price I got *How to Write: Advice and Reflections* by Richard Rhodes and *Telling Time: Angels, Ancestors, and Stories* by Nancy Willard—also on writing. All look good.

Rochester is with me as I sit with my legs down the sofa length as always cuddled on my legs, and I will close now so I can watch a little TV and relax. I wrote a lot more than I intended. The day was lovely and we also went to Mardens and Wal-Mart as always, and I went to Renaissance for Easter cards. I intended seeing Cheryl there for a few minutes, but she was not working today so I left her a note in the office. We went to dinner at the Diner and then shopped at Shaws and came home. How I missed Bookland.

SATURDAY, APRIL 8, 2000

It was rainy in the morning but gradually the sun came out and even now at 5:30 PM it is shining brightly and there is a lot of wind. The sweet

Mallards have been around many times today and the deck is filled with chipmunks, squirrels and all kinds of birds there as well as on feeders. It is wonderful!!

> *Many seeds of suffering have been handed down to us by our ancestors, our parents, and our society. We have to recognize these seeds.*
> —Thich Nhat Hanh

THE INDIVIDUAL AFFIRMATION
I am one of a kind
There is only one spectacular me!
When I was made they broke the mold.
Nobody will ever again have what I have.

—and this poem goes on to say that nobody will be who I am or have my smile, or walk as I do, for I am a unique creation and that all who know me are lucky to have me as a gift.

Imagine being such a positive human being that one could write such things about oneself. I cannot copy it word for word for this book as it is in my journal but the writer goes on to exclaim that the world is a happier and brighter place because of her and that she is thankful for all the things that make her different and for those who are near her. And she relishes that her face in the crowd is the only one who will ever be her.

She reminds me of my mother when she writes that for my Mother often said to me as I left the house that I should be careful and she would add, "Remember, there is only one you." The author of this long lovely poem I have had to paraphrase is Jodi Levy and was in *The Healing Handbook: A Beginners Guide and Journal to Meditation.* I entered the poem in full in this journal because it is so opposite of myself and how I feel about myself and I need to read it often and try to appreciate her lovely positive thoughts without condemning myself for feeling conceited.

I have written this in here because I find it so beautiful. It is from a lovely little book I bought at Mardens. It makes me cry no matter when I read it. I wish I could feel what the young woman that wrote it feels. She loves herself, after the death of her mother when she (the author) was twenty-one, and after being on drugs, having bulimia, and many other things happen to her. She has recovered and is trying to help others. She had such low self-esteem it is why her previous life before now was so tragic. But I cannot read that and believe it for myself, but I want to one day. And that is why I decided to write it out because writing something is important to me, and why I want to continue to read it. How I long to feel about myself as related to that poetic affirmation. Many others feel as I do too. As this journal says at the top of the pages, I am going to "believe—imagine—dream" that one day I can believe that affirmation for myself. Help me, dear Christ.

I have to begin in the heart of my "inner child," the "little girl" within me. She needs healing so much. Help her, help me, dear Christ.

(There is a picture of myself as a little girl glued into my journal at this paragraph.)

MONDAY, APRIL 10, 2000

The little girl on the preceding page makes me cry when I look at her. I finally took this picture down from the side of the refrigerator where Bob hung it many years ago because he said he liked it. She would look at me at my place on the sofa at night when I sat down to relax and often upset me. The picture became dirty (it was 8x10) so I took it down and cut out her little face. Now that she has been in this journal two days she makes me cry much more often. I guess I am so messed up inside. I pray it helps to have her here and the affirmation I wrote two pages previous to her. I feel like she is more secure glued into this journal and not exposed to the outside world.

Every flower is a soul blossoming in Nature
—Gerard DeNerval

This article I have glued into this journal at this point is very important and I plan to do this again soon. I have done similar before about other situations in my life in the past, but I need to do it all again and be very serious and disciplined. The article is titled "Write It Down, Feel Better."

It is well known that writing about something that is bothering you can make you feel better psychologically. Now there is new evidence that it may make you feel better physically too.

In a study of 112 adults with rheumatoid arthritis or chronic asthma, doctors asked two thirds to write about a very upsetting event in their lives. They wrote for 20 minutes a day, three days in a row. The rest just wrote about their plans for the day. At checkups two weeks, two months and four months later, almost half of those who had written about a traumatic experience had marked improvements in their asthma or arthritis—where as over half the others had no change at all.

This is the first study to show that writing about stressful events may actually reduce the symptoms of a chronic illness. Why? Trauma may produce hormone changes that affect long term health and writing about it may help restore balance.

FRIDAY, APRIL 14, 2000

Am at my desk working on my book but took this mini break to glue in this article that has been loose for a long time before I lose it. Will discuss it another time but it is worthy. I have to get back to my writing now.

NIGHT

Worked for hours on my book today. Came downstairs at 8:15 PM. Am now working on the chapter "Trees" but worked on others too in regard to the "Record and Journal" endings. I still have no title but ever since I began writing it I have liked "Beneath the Stars and Trees." As a subtitle possibly this: "A Retreat in the Woods" or "A Woodland Retreat." I think I like the first one better. I have to pray about the entire thing. I am surprised I do not have the title yet but I have been concentrating on writing. My other books though I had the title first. I will write it all out on separate paper and pray and report back in here later about it. Rochester was with me all day. How I love him. He is my Angel. He is in the book, of course! He will be all through it.

Please dear Christ, help me to know what to do about the things that are heavy on my heart. I do not want to write them in here, not yet, anyway. Good nite!

SATURDAY, APRIL 15, 2000

Today is the estimated date of Rochester's birth by the first vet we took him to as a kitten at Rau. Since we could not be certain, I made his birthday on Janna's birthday since she helped me to bring him into our lives. How many times have I written this before, but my love for him is so deep it needs writing again. He is here with me asleep in his soft quilt and I write here in our writing room. I could not live without him. He is my little love.

"We walk through the forests of physical things that are also spiritual things that look on us with affectionate looks."

—Baudelire

SUNDAY, APRIL 16, 2000

We went to Mass and it is Palm Sunday. The readings are extremely long and everyone stands for them. I feel sorry for some of the very old there and the little kids. It maybe takes 20 minutes or longer. (entire time standing) But it was a lovely Mass and we went to Close to Home Restaurant afterwards for breakfast.

After relaxing a bit with Bob and reading the paper and enjoying Rochester, I worked on things for Blue Dolphin. I had to do my drawings over they could not find for my *The Enchantment of Writing*, which was fine, plus Bob made another picture of me as a little girl, scanning the original picture and it turned out great, the picture that is so sweet I write about and a piece of my face is missing. It is not like I am writing about myself, yet it is the little child that lives still within me.

This all took a long time but I wrote accompanying letters and then packaged it all up and it is ready to mail Priority Mail tomorrow plus I sent an e-mail saying it would be there to Chris Wednesday.

It was a beautiful day today—about 70 degrees, but it will be cold again tomorrow. Chester was out on the porch a lot. He loves it—then we were upstairs together too while I did my drawings. We communicate in spirit. It is all blessings. We had a sweet day and a fine evening. Proofread a lot of my chapter on "Rocks." Bob typed too.

(A picture of Christ on the cross is glued at top of page)—I cut this picture from the Jenkintown Methodist Church's newsletter. I want to add color to it but I am not going to and will leave it as is.

I will put this old picture of myself under Jesus. (it is the childhood close-up I spoke of earlier and a piece of the photograph is missing over my left cheek and corner of my left eye and forehead) It all speaks to me on a deeper level when I look into this little tiny girl's eyes. Help me, dear Christ!

We had to send a copy of this picture of me to Blue Dolphin today for my book. Bob made a beautiful copy on special photo paper. This one I will glue in was just on regular paper and did not turn out but I could not throw it away, so I will keep her safe in here.

I am the Mother of all things,
My love is poured out upon the earth.
Be cleansed. Be healed. Be changed.

The above is a prayer from Mary. I visualize her as a forgiving Mother. I imagine her hands covering mine and I hear her say the above lines.

Treating myself like a precious object will make me strong.
—Julia Cameron, *The Artist's Way*

I have entered the above so many times in the front covers of my note books and journals but I cannot seem to grasp the message. It needs to be entered in this journal too. I will enter it during Holy Week. Maybe it will become a truth for me.

This has been a good day writing on my new book. Am working on the chapter "Trees."

TUESDAY, APRIL 18, 2000

A photo of the cover of my new book—but with wrong subtitle and my name not on it. (The photo appears above the writing—It is of *Journal of Love.*)

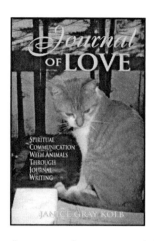

This is a small copy of the cover of my next book that Bob made. He made four, the other three have my name on at the bottom. Lito (at Blue Dolphin) designed it from a photo I took of Rochester and sent it—and I love it! He removed the seam of the window in the middle so it had no interference. The outdoors can be seen clearly through the window. Chester looks so sweet overlooking my papers with writing on. This picture is not as clear or as true in color. Lito just made the subtitle up because he needed one while designing the cover and did not know the real one. The finished cover should be beautiful. I am so thankful my beloved Rochester is on the cover.

Still working on the chapter about "Trees." Corrected some things so did not get as much written as I hoped because I also needed to address and send more Easter cards and they all had notes in them. Bob is typing my book but is slower than last year but I believe he will catch up. Have finally checked two chapters. It is so good to be up in my room writing with my beloved little Chester with me. We are in another world. We speak in silence.

The Mallards are on the porch the majority of the day. We are sure they will mate in a few days. Two males fight over "Mrs." often and one stays with her all the time. Bob is asleep and Chester is asleep here on me as I write. Thank you dear Christ for Rochester and for Bob and for our life together here forevermore. Thank you dear Angels for watching over us.

The peepers are singing every night now and the music is ethereal. I am sure they would approve of this Frog Journal I am using. I have written about them in the book I am writing. Good night now.

When your heart is broken it's hard to feel blessed and protected. All your love energy, all your heart energy leaks out through the break line. You don't feel loved, protected, and guided. You feel drained, tired, exhausted and helpless.

—Melody Beattie, *Finding Your Way Home (a Soul Survival Kit)*

Yes I know.

—Jan

THURSDAY, APRIL 20, 2000

No time to do my writing because of Easter gifts etc. I had to get together for all of Jessica's family and then we had to deliver them after school and we stayed a little while—all outside in the yard. Maxine was not there. Jess is so sweet. They are leaving tomorrow for Pennsylvania for a week or so, so we will not be with them for Easter. We are going to be with George, Val, Janna, Bill and children in Rhode Island who want us to be there. We have to leave super early to make a church service which we want to go to with them, but it will be a lovely day. It is a lot of mileage and six hours driving but worth it. Not a very interesting entry. It is Maundy Thursday and we are staying at home together tonight and feel as spiritual as if we were in church. There is an Angel with me. Rochester is on my lap.

GOOD FRIDAY, APRIL 21, 2000

I did not get any writing done on my book today and that is frustrating. We went to Wolfeboro and I had my eye checkup with Dr. Marsh. He is very nice and we have interesting conversations. He is shy but witty. It went great there and all is well. Will write more about it another time. It is late now. I am thankful. Bob was to have had some blood taken but forgot his forms plus he was not to have eaten last night before it was taken, so he has to go back. He was shocked going over in the car he had forgotten but it is okay. I thought he was prepared.

I was pleased to meet Karen (cannot think of her last name) the nutritionist that Bob had to see some weeks ago. It is too much to write tonight. It is 1:40 AM. But she was very happy to see us and commented right away on my books. More later.

It snowed for hours today heavily but did not accumulate on the ground. We were driving in it all the time. We had a nice evening. lots of Easter cards. I sent so many! Now we received a bunch. So precious to be with Chester all evening on my lap and now he is asleep on my legs. My Angel. The weather is to be bad all weekend. Really not a good time to have to drive to Rhode Island. I love you, dear Christ. I love you, dear Angels.

SATURDAY, APRIL 22, 2000

I write down some thoughts in here by an unknown person from a little clipping I had saved from an unknown source. But I like the spunk of the article. It gives encouragement. It states that we must allow ourselves to write the stories we were meant to write and give ourselves permission to tell. And more importantly give up the vain hope that people will like your work. People like vanilla ice cream. Hope that they love your work or hate it. That they find it exquisite or revolting. It states that Cocteau had the right idea when he said, *"Listen to first criticisms made of your work. Note just what it is about your work that critics don't like and cultivate it. That's the only part of your work that's individual and worth keeping."* It states to throw off the shackles of approval and of wanting to be liked. The minute you capitulate to changing even a single comma to please someone else, or choose one adjective over another to protect a person's feelings, you pull the plug on your own respirator. And that is pretty much a good paraphrase of the thoughts I find very interesting and encouraging.

Spent most of the day wrapping little gifts for all our grandchildren in Rhode Island to take down tomorrow. Observing all of nature outside our windows as I wrapped. So many birds and activities, and new calls. It is snowing again today. I feel so sorry for the Mallards, and peepers. It does not seem that "Mrs." Mallard and her mate have mated yet. They were here again today. These past several weeks they are continually on our porch and on our grounds or out front nearby on the lake. They even rap on the window. "Mrs." does this! But "Mr." did it once too. I am really tired. I do not know how I am going to get up at 5:00 AM tomorrow.

Bob has already fallen asleep. Rochester and I are here together but now we have to sleep too.

SUNDAY—EASTER, APRIL 23, 2000

Christ is Risen!
Hallelujah!
We are going to Rhode Island. I cannot write now and I know I will be too tired when we return, so I will just make this small entry and write more tomorrow. I cannot stand to leave Rochester alone. We will "talk in spirit" to each other while apart.

MONDAY, APRIL 24, 2000

Every flower is a soul blossoming in nature
—Gerard DeNerval

As I entered that I suddenly had a rush of memory because of the word "blossoming." As a little girl I was in a Brownie Troop and we each had to have another name pertaining to nature. At this writing I cannot remember whether the name was given to me or that I chose it for myself, but my Brownie name was "Blossom." And I loved it! Perhaps that is a message to me this very day. I think it is. I am to "blossom." I surely need to.

LATER

I just had something come to mind that I do not believe I ever entered in any journal. Since none of my family is interested in my writing and books, I will enter it in here to keep for myself. Leslie (and this was unusual because family never mentions my books or shows any interest) gave a report in college and used my book *Compassion for All Creatures* and she said her teachers and others showed great interest.

Then soon after I went into "Made on Earth," my favorite store in Wolfeboro, and there was a new saleswoman. We got into a discussion on books because I was buying two and I told her about my *Compassion* that was on their shelves. She was so happy I did because her daughter (in high school in Connecticut or Massachusetts, I forget which) also used my book *Compassion* for study and gave a report on it too. The woman said they both loved my book and her daughter's report went really well. It all made me feel so good that I am helping the animals.

We saw both Mr. and Mrs. Mallard and they were on our deck—and stayed and welcomed the bread I fed them. I was so glad to see them. This means they have not mated yet if it is as it was last year, for once they mate she begins to come around to us alone until she has her babies and then they are always with her. "Mr." guards "Mrs." now to be on watch for other male mallards, while "Mrs." eats the bread crumbs and loves them. Also witnessed another fight mid-air between "Mr." and other male mallards. There are a lot of males hanging around. Six were together in the lake today and out front. Poor little "Mrs." But her mate guards her.

So many new birds at the feeders and a pair of Mourning Doves are always here. They are ground feeders and feed right along with the chipmunks side by side. Even though it is cold and even when it snowed Friday and Saturday, the peepers were still singing. What a precious thing it is to live life here with all these dear creatures and the lake and the woods.

We had a wonderful time in Rhode Island Sunday at George's and Val's, and Janna, Bill and children were there. We went to church and it was beautiful and the message spoke to my heart. Will write about it all later. We drove in the rain all the way down and all the way back. Left at 6:30 AM and got there in the church by 9:45 AM and the service began at 10 AM.

TUESDAY, APRIL 25, 2000

Working on my chapter "Trees" still. There were several days at the end of the week I could not work on it because of preparing gifts etc. to take to Rhode Island. I am back writing and it feels so good. Rochester is with me. Rochester is always with me.

Precious moments watching the Mallard couple today and the male Mallards who try to interfere. I will write about it in more detail tomorrow and it will be in this book I am writing.

Left loving messages on George's and Val's answering machine yesterday and today about our time with them on Sunday and about buying all the new furniture we bought today with gift certificate for Ames they gave us for Christmas.

Bob arranged all the new chairs in a semi-circle on the lawn; four Adirondack chairs and ten other type green chairs, more straight, all alike. It was a sunny day and I took picture of them so I can send them to George and Val. Also included the beautiful orange tulips in the picture that they gave us for Easter. There will be plenty of seating outdoors this summer.

WEDNESDAY, APRIL 26, 2000

Why do I frequently need to protect myself from those who say they love me?
—Ashleigh Brilliant

I am glueing below here in my Frog Journal a little article from Country Journal that tells of a CD popular on college campuses right now that has a very old fashioned sound. The music is not electrified or amplified—in fact it is not played on instruments at all. "The Sounds of North American Frogs" (Smithsonian Folkways Recordings) features 85 frog calls and 53 different species with informative narration by herpetologist Charles Bogart. It is to listen to for relaxing enjoyment, or to study up on the various frog calls. You can then use your new aural knowledge to help you identify the noisy dwellers of your local pond. I will record the e-mail address to check it out. It costs $14.00. WWW. si.edu/folkways.

This seems appropriate to store here in my Frog Journal in case I am interested in the future. I did make my own tape of our peepers several years ago placing the tape recorder by the lake. When I walked down to place it there the singing stopped, actually it gradually stopped the closer I got to the water. As I left with the peepers in silence, the further away I walked the peepers gradually began to sing again. By the time I reached the porch they were in full swing once more. Funny!! There was a repeat of the entire thing when I went down first to turn the tape over, and then finally to collect the tape recorder. It is a good tape. I remember I sent a copy to Bobby too to listen to at bedtime. I will have to get my own copy again although hardly need it now with the peepers singing every night and to almost dawn. At 5 AM when I wakened they were still going strong this morning.

I thought it appropriate to glue in this photo (a photo is on opposite page) of my two frogs since I am discussing *Peepers* in my Frog Journal.

Janna made the flowered frog for me that Bob named Gorfa—which is "a frog" spelled backwards. Jessica and girls gave me the green frog I named "Ribbit." I have had both several years. Sent a print of this and one similar to Don Richards today since he gave me this frog journal.

I felt inspired and took a break to write to the address in the front of this journal to request a catalog. I told them this journal had been bought for me in Juneau, Alaska. I wrote a nice letter saying this one is lovely and much more. We will see if they answer. Hope so.

> *To bring anything into your life, imagine that it is already there.*
> —Richard Bach

> *Argue for your limitations and they are yours*
> —Richard Bach

> *I say unto you: a man must have chaos yet within him*
> *to be able to give birth to a dancing star.*
> —Nietzche

THURSDAY, APRIL 27, 2000

Imagine what your life would be like if you knew that:—You are more lovable and beautiful than you know. You are more powerful and important than you think.

> —Dr. Louise Hart, *On the Wings of Self Esteem*

There were other points made by the author but these spoke to me.

FRIDAY, APRIL 28, 2000

I spent all day writing on my book or finishing a chapter, I should say. Have been working on the chapter on "Trees" for some time (a week maybe) and that is because I keep adding things and I changed some. Actually I still have some finishing touches and then the writing of the "Reflect and Journal" part that closes each chapter. It has been a joy to be doing it.

Inside yourself is a memory of a child who was not accepted and was hurt. Use your imagination to receive and embrace that child, and reassure it with your adult knowledge, understanding, and compassion. Give it what it needs.

—*On the Wings of Self Esteem*

*A prophet is not without honour,
but in his own country,
and among his own kin,
and in his own house.*

—Mark 6:4

"For the rest of my life there are two days that will never again trouble me. The first day is yesterday"—and author Og Mandino states that yesterday has passed away with all its blunders and tears and defeats and is no longer in my control. "The other day is tomorrow," he says. That will have its dangers, mystery, pitfalls and until the sun rises again he claims he has no stake in tomorrow for it has not yet been born. Those words in paraphrase are from The Return of the Ragpicker.

If I can only soon adapt this into the philosophy of my life.

The Mallards were here again as usual and they are so dear. "Mr." stays so close to "Mrs." guarding and watching. He waits while she eats the bread crumbs I throw them and the seed on the ground. I talk to them and I notice that they frequently respond to what I say silently. Today before I could go outside a drama played out outside. "Mr." and "Mrs." came onto the porch. Both at different times knocked on the window. So cute! "Mrs." began to eat when suddenly two males came from the lake from the left side of the house. As they approached "Mr." took off at them and the three males flew off with a fight going on in the air between two, and one was "Mr." fending off these guys who were trying to steal "Mrs." I watched as "Mrs." ate and then another mallard "couple" came strolling up our front beach and across the grass. She kept eating as they approached. Never did the male bother "Mrs." Apparently his interest was only in the female with him and he began to put his beak into her feathers and she got seemingly upset and flew off with him following her. Our "Mrs." kept eating. But I neglected to mention that when this couple first arrived on the deck "Mrs." stopped eating and kept opening and closing her beak as if upset or calling for help, yet I did not hear any sound. She was obviously agitated that this other couple was on "her" deck and also that her male was not with her. I sent out little loving messages. It was all so interesting. I wanted to comfort her. After this couple flew off, eventually "Mr." returned. They just stayed briefly then, then toddled off to the side of our house and down onto the beach and into the water. It was all quite a drama, that I have not captured as well as I would have liked here. I feel so honored "Mrs." loves it here, and "Mr." But "Mrs." will stay and that is wonderful. I am communicating with her with results.

SATURDAY, APRIL 29, 2000

Had time to work on my book several hours despite the fact on Saturdays Bob and I also spend time together and do not work all day. But he was doing some typing for me and also some cleaning up outside, and actually it was more than just a few hours that I got to write. Felt good about all I am capturing.

When will my *Journal of Love* be finished? It is six months late. It will be lovely when it is completed I just know and worth the wait.

SUNDAY, APRIL 30, 2000

Went to Mass and that was meaningful. Also to see the beautiful lilies on the altar and six of them were given in memory of my parents, Uncle Elmer, "Friar Francis" McGeary, Barry Greene and Dad Kolb as we always do. I usually cut out their names and glue them in my journal (did that too in my other journal at Christmas), but we did not get a program at Easter because we were in Rhode Island. So I mention the names here today after seeing the lovely lilies.

We ate at Close to Home Restaurant and that was fun and delicious (had their wonderful country fries and toasted bagel as usual) and then after spending time together reading the paper and talking we separated briefly and Bob did a bit more typing in the Birchgrove and I wrote some more on my book. Then the rest of the day we were together. My beloved little Rochester is always with me, my dear little silent companion of love.

Monday, May 1, 2000

May Day! Wrote all day. It was glorious. Rochester ever with me.

> *Who bends a knee*
> *Where violets grow*
> *A hundred secret*
> *Things shall know.*
>
> —Anonymous, for my Mother Violet

Monday, May 1, 20000—May Day

Have ordered this tape (picture of it glued on page) from my Writer's Digest Book Club by two of my favorite authors at this segment of my life. The tape is *A Conversation on The Writing Life—Ideas and Inspiration for Anyone Who Wants to Write* by Julia Cameron and Natalie Goldberg. Natalie rates first for she came along first in 1986 as I began to write and Rochester entered my life. I have written that in the wrong order. First beloved Rochester came into my life and then I began to write my books, even though I had always written in journals. I bought Natalie's *Writing Down the Bones* and loved it and have read it again and again and it has helped me so much. I wrote to her back then and received a nice reply. I have all of her books, all read multiple times and I will continue to read them for they inspire. I own another tape by her called *Writing the Landscapes of Your Mind* and it is her Minnesota Workshop. I have not heard it yet or any tapes bought recently. There is no time in winter and Spring when I am always working on a book. I will save them till summer. I have a tape by Julia also—*Reflections on the Artists Way.* I have three of her books and they have all been read more than once also. They are the ones mentioned on the previous page in the write-up about her. I have mentioned both these writers at length in my *The Echantment of Writing.* They both live in New Mexico so I guess they decided to team up for this tape. How nice! I look forward to all three tapes soon.

I am enjoying working on the chapter "Gardens" for my book. I am including a lot of nice things. Worked on it all of today plus rechecked some things Bob typed. Everything reads very well. I keep getting new ideas to add, but that is good!

Mr. and Mrs. Mallard were around again as always, and on Saturday and Sunday too. They let me come quite close to feed them. It seems they have not mated as yet, unless this is an unusual male who is sticking by her after they did. We just have to keep watching. They are so sweet. I look at them as she eats and he keeps guard and wonder what they are thinking. They are very dear to me—especially Mrs. But he is being dutiful now and I cannot be upset with him if he leaves her after they have mated because it is the way God created him. But why? I am thankful they are in my life.

TUESDAY, MAY 2, 2000

Working on my book. It is wonderful to be writing it. Rochester can be out on the screened in porch more now due to the sun and weather warming up a bit.

This is the first day the Mallards did not come around in weeks, unless we missed them, and I doubt that. Perhaps they have mated and we will soon see "Mrs." here alone.

My heart is so hurt by three whom I love who are close to me but I do not want to write about it in here. Bob and I discuss it. Jessica and family are back from Jenkintown as of Sunday night. We have talked several times and she is so loving. Janna, too!

WEDNESDAY, MAY 3, 2000

I wrote all day and the chapter on "Gardens" is getting longer. I like it. Spent time finding a lot of my poems related to flowers etc. also. I love writing so much.

Chester was on the porch a lot and I miss him. It is because it has just become warm enough for us to be out there and it feels lovely to him as it does to me. But he comes up and cuddles on my lap and lays on my desk often and I go down to be with him. He is coaxing us both to be outdoors. As always he runs in the bedroom so we can be together. So precious.

Had a long e-mail from Dennis yesterday and I answered. He is such a faithful friend.

A call came today and my new glasses are ready. We have decided to go and pick them up first in Rochester tomorrow and then go over to Sanford from there. They may take some getting used to. This picture above of the sweet cat (pasted on the upper right hand corner of the journal page) must be a relative of Chester's, but then Chester is an Angel—sent to me. Thank you, dear Christ.

Yesterday was "Remembrance Day" (May 2) for all the dear Holocaust victims. All week is being dedicated to them in remembrance but Tuesday was the significant day. All week people are taking turns reading aloud the thousands of names of people killed in the holocaust. I do not know where it is taking place but it is continuous. What a beautiful thing to do, to say each victim's name aloud. It makes me cry just writing about it.

THURSDAY, MAY 4, 2000

Got this purple ink pen at Mardens today to only use on days pertaining to my Mother when writing in my journals. I will just use it now to say it is for "Violet" and that we bought a wonderful "Lilac" plant today that will grow to be eighteen feet tall and ten feet wide. It is the state flower of New Hampshire. I have wanted lilac for so long! Its name is "The Donald Wyman Lilac."

A nice day in Sanford. Did not get any writing done, of course. Went to all our usual stores and library and had fun together. Went to the Upper Storey Bookstore again. Nice, but cannot compare to Bookland. Stood with my face to the window at Bookland gazing in at the emptiness and it made me cry again. We had a good dinner at Jerry's Diner and are having a lovely evening here with Rochester. Enjoyed "Who Wants to be a Millionaire" with Regis Philbin. Am tired. So good to have my little one on my lap.

FRIDAY, MAY5, 20000

Had hoped to write all day but Janna called saying they would be here for the weekend and so we had to straighten up and clean instead because we had been so involved with my writing and Bob's typing of it and also his outside work in between black fly attacks (it is that season!) that we needed some straightening up in the kitchen area. I am so anxious to see Janna and Bill and family! I am losing a day of writing I had counted on and am so filled with things to put down on paper, but I will catch up soon. We had nice relaxing evening though, Bob , Chester and I. Janna was to arrive at the Inn later tonight.

During this period with company here over the weekend (Janna, Bill and family and our Clancys), we have not had our sweet Mallards on the deck because of all the human activity. But glorious birds are returning to the feeders and are here continuously. Will write about them soon. I cannot wait to return to writing tomorrow, but we had a beautiful weekend.

MONDAY, MAY 8, 2000

The "lilac" or "violet" ink I used on a recent previous page is too light and looks like it already faded. Very unusual it would do that. I will not use it in my journals but go back to my usual violet pen which is lovely that I only use on my Mother Violet's special days.

Have been working on my book all day and still on the chapter about "Gardens." I keep thinking of new things to include in it and I still am not finished and will continue tomorrow. I cannot wait. I love writing this book, but then I have felt that way about each book I have written. Each chapter I have done in this one I have enjoyed doing too. I still have more to write. I will probably write about "birds" next.

Rochester is loving being able to be on the porch again. It is so good for him. Every once in a while when he does go on the porch he then comes upstairs a very little while after to cuddle with me on my lap or to be on my desk and papers as I write, then he leaves—then returns. Then stays with me as always and as he does all the months of the year when it is too cold to be on the screened-in-porch. He is my Angel in soft fur. This is our room. It is Holy. He is so precious. And all evening he lies on my legs as I sit on the sofa with them stretched down the length, and he sleeps like that in bed with me too. He is my blessed Angel.

TUESDAY, MAY 9, 2000

The Mallards were back yesterday and today. Also Bluejays for the first time in so long, four of them! So beautiful! All on our deck. And two male Baltimore Orioles, but I only see one female. The males at one point were fighting like the male Mallards do. And two Goldfinch (we think this is correct), male and females, and our Mourning Doves, Sparrows (Chipping), Nuthatches and Chickadees. Also the Grackles and even the Crows. Such singing, noise and activity out front on our feeders, deck and lawn. It is so wonderful—not to mention the other birds I do not know plus the little squirrels and chipmunks. Incredible! Exciting!

LATER

I will write more about it when I have more time, but today in the mail I received my manuscript of *The Enchantment of Writing* with all the pictures now in place! It looks absolutely beautiful!! It has 296 pages and it looks incredible! I read passages of it and it makes my cry. It is such treasure to me, to have recorded all that I have. I do not know how I did it. I know my Angels helped me every day all the way, and that means especially my beloved Angel Rochester—my constant companion and inspiration and little love. Thank you, dear Christ and Rochester and Mary and my Angels. I look at it and am in awe that I wrote it! Such details! I could never have done it without supernatural help. I just kept my pencil on the paper and wrote my heart out. I pray it will not be held up in anyway as *Journal of Love* has been. All it needs now is Bob's hymn.

LATER 5 PM

A horrible thunder and lightening storm came up out of the blue and I stopped writing at my desk to sit back in my arm chair so I could hold Chester. He was afraid and it was understandable. It was awful! I get nervous too. We cuddled together. It just died down and stopped so he is here on the floor on my feet partially as I entered this.

I have been working on a section of the chapter of "Gardens" and it is the section on "grass." I have just finished but have not reread it. It includes sweet things and now I am writing about "rain." That has some memories of Joe Clancy in it. I decided to write about "rain" because it is raining and has been and I get the full feeling for it.

So many birds. Took time to feed Mrs. Mallard. When I called to her as she began to walk away, she turned and ran across the lawn to me like a little child and stood at my feet while I fed her. It made me have tears. Her mate was very nearby but there was another male mallard there and he was fending him off. They pecked at each other's chests. He really guards "Mrs." and they keep making little noises because they are upset with the intruder. He likes her to be fed by me obviously—and patiently waits. I try to get him to eat too. Occasionally he will if he is more relaxed, but not with another male there. The birds at our feeders are amazing.

Dear Christ, I need your help. You know what I am talking about. Please help me. And thank you for Bob's and Chester's perfect health and appointments. Amen.

WEDNESDAY, MAY 10, 2000

I learned to think of God as a woman and by that simple experience
I discovered I could begin to think of God.
—Jan O'Reillly

I have no parents—I make the heavens and earth my parents.
I have no home—I make awareness my home.
—14th century Samurai

Poetry is the voice of the soul.
—Carolyn Forche

Your sacred space is where you find yourself again and again.
—Joseph Cambell

Yes, I say Amen and Amen to that! Rochester does also.

I believe that my work is worthy of its own space,
which is worthy of the name Sacred.
—Jan Phillips

Worked all day on my book. Still in the chapter on "Gardens." I love what I am writing, but will anyone else? Even my family does not read what I write.

A rainforest day and I loved it. We settled down to watch *West Wing,* and it was supposed to have an unusual finale (we like the show so much) and lightning struck during a big storm and blew out our dish or whatever it is that brings us the main channels. So disappointing. Bob put on some movie on the other channels that worked (not the three main ABC, NBC,and so forth) and then we watched CNN. We lost our favorite programs. I hate to miss our New Hampshire news and Ted Koppel. Now to some reading. Rochester is ever here on my legs.

THURSDAY, MAY 11, 2000

There is such a thing as sacred idleness,
the cultivation of which is now fearfully neglected.
—George MacDonald

LISTEN

Listen!
    Tiny birds compose their songs
        even on a morning of gray—
           and hearts are brightened
            and heightened
In the dawn of a new day.

Jan

Just rediscovered this poem I wrote in July 1999. I do not think I have seen it since then. Bob had it on a paper to type. I will be writing a chapter on "birds" soon so I think I will use it.

Worked all day on my book. It was a joy. I keep adding things to this "Garden" chapter.

FRIDAY, MAY 12, 2000

If of thy mortal goods thou art bereft,
And from thy slender store two loaves alone
    to thee are left,
Sell one, and with the dole
Buy hyacinths to feed the soul.
—Gubistan of Moslin Eddin Saadi
(a Mohammedan Sheik)

There is serene and settled majesty to woodland scenery that enters into the soul and delights and elevates it, and fills it with noble inclinations.
—Washington Irving

There is a poem that speaks to me written by John Moffitt. I say "yes, yes" to it each time I read it. He writes how if we are to look at anything how we must look at a thing long. He writes how we must be the thing we see. Not just use words to describe the thing. He states, "You must be the dark snakes of stems and ferny plumes of leaves." He desires that we enter in to the small silences between the leaves and his words are very lovely and this poem is about my reactions to many things in nature that touch me so deeply. The name of his poem is "To Look at Anything."

MONDAY MAY 15, 2000

BENEATH THE STARS AND TREES

Beneath the stars and trees
   I am alive!
      I thrive in these woods
         filled with wildlife and flowers,
  and sunshine streaking through
    the tall firs and pines
       birds flitting from branch to branch
         and on the vines,
  flying in and out feasting on seed
    at the feeders.
       And red squirrels eating perched
        with the birds—
  and tiny chipmunks claiming
    the fall-out from the abundance,
       and Mallards that run to greet me
        and wait by my front door.
Where else is life like this,
    that one's dear friend who comes to call
      is a wild duck?
        And the rocks murmur when I pass!
I walk the soft green grass to lake's edge
    to behold the setting sun.

And when shadows descend
and twilight comes—
the peepers serenade
from the watery cove—
and I gaze up at the heavens
to feel the moonglow on my face.
Within the green cottage a loving man
and a gentle cat await my return.
Yes, there is a place—
beneath the stars and trees.

Jan

I began this poem on Saturday night in bed and it poured out. I was tired and let it alone. Last night after midnight I looked at it again and added several lines about Bob and Rochester and rearranged the lines. I record it now and I will use it in the front of my new book by the same title. It was waiting inside me to be written. It just flowed! It amazes me and I am so thrilled to have it.

LATER

A million sparkling stars
fill the vast arc—
a sight incomprehensible
as I stand alone in the darkness.

I have written the verse at the bottom of the opposite page to be inserted into my poem after the line that reads—
"to feel the moonglow on my face."

I love the poem so much but in reading it a number hours after writing it in here I felt I wanted to say more about the stars.

I changed two more things. Instead of the word "streaking" (5th line) I will use "streaming." And I have added to line 16. It will read—"and wait by my front door."

Now it is just as I wish the poem to be. I will write it now anew even though it is long so I can have it perfectly in this journal.

BENEATH THE STARS AND TREES

Beneath the stars and trees
    I am alive!
        I thrive in these woods
            filled with wildlife and flowers,
and sunshine streaming through
    the tall firs and pines—
        birds fluttering from branch to branch
           and on the vines—
flying in and out feasting on seed
    at the feeders.
        And red squirrels eating perched
           with the birds—
and tiny chipmunks claiming
    the fall-out from the abundance,
        and mallards that run to greet me
           and wait by my front door.
Where else is life like this,
    that one's dear friend who comes to call
        is a wild duck?
           and the rocks murmur when I pass!
I walk the soft grass to lake edge
    to behold the setting sun.
        And when shadows descend
           and twilight comes—
the peepers serenade
    from the watery cove
        and I gaze up at the heavens
           to feel the moonglow on my face.
A million sparkling stars
    fill the vast arc—
        a sight incomprehensible
           as I stand alone in the darkness.
Within the green cottage a loving man
    and a gentle cat await my return.
        Yes, there is a place—
           beneath the stars and trees.

                                      Jan
                                      May 15, 2000

TUESDAY, MAY 16, 2000

Good morning, Journal and world. It is a glorious day out. It is still morning and the Mallards (Mr. and Mrs.) have already been here three times. I feed them. "Mrs." runs to me! So sweet! I want to get busy writing on my book so I am going upstairs. Rochester is waiting for me.

LATER

I totally finished the chapter on "Gardens." I kept adding and adding to it so it took longer—but I love all I have included. I have to read it over completely.

It has so many personal things in it tucked in amongst the flowers.

Mr. and Mrs. are here again and again throughout the day. I fed them four or five times today. They are so sweet, and he is eating more. She still runs to me when she sees me. They both knock on the front window. It is wonderful!

Tomorrow is Bob's appointment in Laconia. I have not written about it in here on purpose. Dear Christ, I thank you in advance for the perfect results. Thank you, dear Christ.

WEDNESDAY, MAY 19, 2000

Today is Bob's appointment at 12:15 PM. Thank you, dear Christ, for Bob's perfect health and prostate.

TUESDAY, MAY 23, 2000

I am so sorry I have not written in here since Wednesday. It was all too much. I will write things soon but I just needed to put some words down here in my lovely journal.

SATURDAY, MAY 27, 2000

Dear Christ—I need your help! Oh you know. Please help me.

TUESDAY, MAY 30, 2000

Today is Janna's 31st birthday. I cannot believe it. We called her around noon.

Today is my beloved Rochester's fourteenth birthday, a day assigned him because Janna helped me to get him that day fourteen years ago on June 23rd. I have always been grateful to her and I love her so, but she never mentions Rochester—not even today. It hurts me so much. None of my children mention him. Why? I am remembering again that when Janna was small (well, she is always small!), she could not say her middle name "Rebecca." She pronounced it "Recca-becca." We still often call her Janna Recca-Becca." She is a beautiful gift and precious daughter.

Tomorrow I will write more about Chester. I will celebrate him all week —but actually I celebrate his life and presence every single day.

My chest is all tight in the middle tonight yet I thought all fear of the thing that is plaguing me was dismissed. Subconsciously perhaps the tenseness has caused this. Please dear Christ help me, and Mary and Dad and Mother.

I will write more another time about Bob's wonderful results of the biopsy on his prostate—but also about the way our book store on-line is growing. We mailed off seven books today, and ordered late Saturday night, four ordered Sunday, and two ordered today! Good night, dear little Rochester, lying here in bed on my legs as always, his sweet face asleep on his little front legs that reach out to touch my hand. I will hold his little paws now as I always do. How nice this picture is on the upper corner of this page as I write about Chester. It was the first cat picture on the Friskie cans of cat food I bought for him. This was on the large size of "mixed grill." I loved it that the cat was orange. They have changed the picture twice since then.

Good night dear little Rochester, my Angel and little beloved, precious one who watches over me. Happy, happy Birthday.

—AN ASIDE—   JUNE 10, 2008 POSTSCRIPT

I used to cut the pictures of the handsome little cats off the labels of the Friskies Cat Food for years and keep them in a little box. I would glue them onto the upper right-hand corners of my journals. Very nice.

FRIDAY JUNE 9, 2000

I have not written in here even though I wanted to because there was so much I wanted to write I gave up. I am sad inside because of a number of things but writing my book helps me so much. I have finished the chapter on "Birds" (124 written pages) this past week and now am working on a chapter on "Journals." I have to get back to work on it.

No one can make you feel inferior without your consent.

—Eleanor Roosevelt

If you can imagine it, you can achieve it. If you can dream it, you can become it.

—Wm. Arthur Ward

Sacred space and sacred time and something joyous to do is all we need. Almost anything then becomes a continuous and increasing joy.

—Joseph Campbell

TUESDAY, JUNE 13, 2000

Toward early morning I had a dream. These past months I have barely been able to remember any dreams at all, yet I know I am dreaming and often have fragments left, but they slip away too. But I woke with this one fairly intact. The other night, Friday I think, we saw a movie in which there was a woods and a cabin. It was a frightening movie about the devil. But in this dream the same woods was there and the clearing in front of the old cabin. It was identical. I went to the door and Dr. Ritsert answered and welcomed me in *(an aside to readers—Dr. Ritsert was Bob's and my Pedodontic instructor when we attended Temple University School of Dentistry [and Oral Hygiene] and later Bob worked for him after graduating and eventually Bob bought his practice and Dr. Ritsert retired)*. Mrs. Ritsert was in bed but not because she was ill. She was happy and just relaxing. She welcomed me with such joy and I went over to her and we embraced. It was all so nice. There was someone in the next room but I never saw them. That is all there was to the dream but it was very clear.

I am sure I dreamed about Effie and Ernest Ritset because while in Sanford Thursday and at the library Bob and I got some books from the "free" book case. There was a set of Winnie the Pooh books in paperback and I immediately said to Bob that they made me think of the Ritserts, because Dr. Ritsert had given me his set of Winnie the Pooh books when they moved and some time before they died. It is so sad the Ritserts are gone. I have treasured their books. They are hardbacks. We talked some more about them lovingly and that was that—then five nights later I dream about them so vividly. I do not ever remember dreaming about them before. It is all so strange. If the dream has meaning I do not know it yet. But it was lovely to see them again Why five nights later? I will have to think about it and pray about it more. I was anxious to record it before I forgot it.

I did not have a chance to say I love the little picture of Dahlia Bob made for me from a larger print Janna sent. Bob made a 5x7 for us and several others and this little one for this journal. She looks so sweet. She had a graduation at Nursery School last week and also she had her hair cut. She looks so pretty. I wanted her little face in here—dear little granddaughter. I love her dearly, and Janna—and Bill too, are so proud of her. She is four and three quarters years old.

Today the cover of my book of *Journal of Love* came—or I believe that is what is in the big flat cardboard. I wanted to wait until tomorrow. I will explain later

Wednesday, June 14, 2000

The cover for my *Journal of Love* is absolutely beautiful!! It makes me cry to see my beloved little Rochester there on the cover. Bob and I are overwhelmed by it. It is perfect. He looks so precious, and the back cover is a pale muted green, so lovely, where comments are. The color ties in with the front for trees, etc—can be seen outside as Rochester sits in the window of my desk. It looks like he is outdoors. The frame of the window does not show.

Thursday, June 15, 2000

We had a lot of book orders which was wonderful so Bob did all the computer work and I did all the packaging and wrapping in tissue with little notes inside as always. We mailed six books!! Our business is doing so well and it is fun. Bob and I had a nice evening together with Chester and Isabelle. We picked Isabelle up at the Inn yesterday for Jessica and family are going down to Jenkintown. Jessica is taking down gifts for us for Tim (graduation and birthday), Ryan (confirmation), Bob G. (birthday) and Colleen, (graduation)

Tim graduated tonight and that is hard to believe. We called and talked to him in late afternoon and had a nice time.

FRIDAY, JUNE 16, 2000

I am on the screened in porch. I will write more later. I have made coffee (Bob usually does that) and so I will make a cup and return to write in here later. The sun is out after days of no sun, it is warmer (it has been like winter) and as always, the birds are singing!

9:45 AM

I made some potato salad, the first this year. It is in the fridge getting cold. Also placed an order for our vegetarian Canadian Bacon at the Health store to pick up next week. Chester is here with me, beloved little one, and Isabelle is out on a long chain under a tree.

NOON

The potato salad is incredible! It turned out so good. I must have done everything right. Just had a dish, my first food—breakfast and lunch, and worth waiting for.

3:10 PM

I am taking a break to be outside on the porch a few minutes. I have been up in my room working on the ending of my chapter on "Journals" and I am nearing the end. Chester was up there with me taking his nap on his quilt and the breezes were blowing in on us, but it is a terribly hot sunny day—the first in so, so long. I like the "Journal" chapter. I am finishing the "Reflect and Journal" part after adding three new poems on "Journaling" I wrote this week, each one written after I was in bed at night.

9:30 PM

Sat on the porch till dark—about 8:50 PM. Isabelle was in the house all afternoon where it was cooler, but I put her out again around 6 PM for about two hours. She loves it outdoors. When I am out there with her she is free and I do not use the chain. We are all inside now and I am so happy I finished my chapter. I will begin a new one tomorrow. Am nearing the end. Even though the window is open it is hot in the house here. Rochester is stretched out on the cool wood of the kitchen table and Isabelle is on the linoleum floor instead of the carpet.

SATURDAY, JUNE 17, 2000

I am out on the porch with coffee and it is 8:30 AM. Isabelle is outside and Rochester is here with me. The breezes are blowing but it is supposed to be a hot day. Now it is lovely. The porch is so lovely to have— to be able to sit here and write and read. It is unusual that yesterday was the first day I could use the porch. The weather has been cold.

3:05 PM

We had a horrible thunder storm come up suddenly at 2:20 PM while we were outside. I brought Chester and Isabelle inside right away then gathered up my writing things. It was so violent and branches are down all over the yard and the winds were high and the electricity went off four times but fortunately stayed on. I just pray it does not go off. Now it is calm and rain and winds have stopped but it is still dark and dreary out.

SUNDAY, JUNE 18, 2000

RX—FOR PEACE—REPEAT DAILY!

Journaling into the night
    oft times in tears
        feeling the weight
            of all my fears—
                all that has gone wrong—
                    all that took my song—
I write and write
    telling the smooth white pages
        all that hides—
            all that abides—
                in the secret recesses
                  of my heart.

And in time
   there is a lightness of being,
      a gradual freeing.
I Pause—
   and in the sacrament of the moment
      having released the past
         breathing freely at last—
            I sigh—
               and give thanks.

                                          Jan

                                 JUNE 12, 2000

I will use this poem in the chapter on journaling in the new book I
am writing and nearing completion on—*Beneath the Stars and Trees—
There Is a Place.*

                        JOURNAL SPEAKING

I am your journal—
   a waiting receptacle
      for all that floats
         from out your pen—
Capturing notes
   directly from your heart—
      holding them in utmost secrecy
         upon my pages,
Protecting them in the now
   and for all ages.
         Writings that are fragments
            of your inner being—
Spread across my whiteness,
   for your seeing—
      an extension
         of self
               in clear view—
Revealing a deeper dimension
   to all that is you.

Journal and pen—
    your transport taken
       to ken

           Jan

           JUNE 15, 2000

Open your journal
    and on pages of white—
Write all your joys—
    and too your "dark night"

Pour out your heart—
    in your journal of choice,
In releasing your words—
    you capture your voice.

           Jan

           JUNE 15, 2000

I am using the previous two poems also in my chapter on journal keeping in my book I am writing.

           WEDNESDAY, JUNE 21, 2000

STARS

S prinkled across the heavens of night—
T rillions of infinitesimal dots of light
A stonish seekers
R everently
S ubdued.

FULL MOON

M ajestically suspended in blackness
O pulently beauteous
O racularly mysterious.
N onplussed we gaze skyward

FLOWERS

F loral beauty
L avishly abounds
O verlooking the lake—
W here birds and butterflies
E nhance the gardens as
R egal appreciators
S ublime.

TREES

T enderly shading
R oads and gardens
E legantly standing watch—
E nergizing earth and life
S acredly.

The five poems on these pages are "acrostic poems" I wrote to use in the book I am writing. They were fun and unusual to write and I was inspired to write them after reading *A Crow Doesn't Need a Shadow* by Lorraine Ferra sent to me by Jeanne Quinn.

FRIDAY, JUNE 23, 2000

ROCHESTER

R eflective and rare.
O verwhelmingly patient and precious—
C ompassionate, constant, contemplative and cherished.
H onorable, humble, beloved friend—
E nlightened and empowering encourager—
S acred, sagacious supporter—
T ender and thoughtful confidant
E minent and everlasting Angel—
R ochester—renowned, radiant, remarkable companion.

Written to honor you—   Jan
and in thanksgiving   June 23, 2000
for the day you came into my life—
June 23, 1986

HARRY

H arry—handsome, honest helper—
A lso known as
R ochester.
R eassuring soulmate—
Y ielding, loving advocate.

Jan
June 24, 2000

Partake of nature daily
for it is the food
that nourishes the soul.

—Anon

RAIN

R ushing rapidly downward
A ffectionately administering to earth,
I ndespensale ingredient for life —
N ourishing, necessary cleansing of worth.

Jan
June 25, 2000

My grief was too deeply rooted to be cured with words.

—Orinda

This speaks of how it felt to be betrayed last June.

THURSDAY, JUNE 29,2000

After the rain a poem came to me tonight.

THE GIANTS

Thunder stomps through the woods
Lightening crackles out its path—
Wildlife hides in the shadows—
Till the passing of the wrath.

Jan

MONDAY, JULY 3, 2000

A number of people I love have shown us total indifference lately to both Bob and me that I can only interpret it as lack of love and it hurts me very much.

Bob does not seem to care and gives me pep talks about us only having each other and Chester and basically that is true. But this indifference from these others is so hurtful. I do not want to write in more detail. Maybe just writing this will help me not to be bothered by it. I will give it all to Jesus in my prayers.

TUESDAY, INDEPENDENCE DAY

Still yet another thing happened today that ties in exactly with what I wrote in the previous entry involving those we love. It was very hurtful and not understandable and involved someone else in addition to those I wrote anonymously about in the July 3rd entry. I just do not understand and Bob does not either. But he laughs about it, but it makes me sad.

WEDNESDAY, JULY 5, 2000

BOOKS

B eneficence awaits
O ccasions of reading
O ffering opportunities
K inship to the
S acrosanct.

JGK

We sent out seven mailers of books today for our bookshop with nine books in them. Since May 17 we have sent out 101 books! (on July 4th —100 books in 49 days [7 weeks]). It is wonderful! I love being a book shop owner. I always wanted to own a book store and now we do. Rochester is co-owner too and keeps company with all the books on the shelves high around our screened in porch awaiting sale. He is the guardian angel. I worked on my chapter about the book shop all afternoon after I finished packaging the books and writing the notes, (and gift wrapping the books) and finished all but the "Reflect and Journal" portion at end of chapter and the adding of two poems I cannot find yet. It was a work of love as is the entire book. It felt good to get back to writing after not being able to be up at my desk since Thursday due to things pertaining to going to Rhode Island Saturday and then being with Clancys here over the 4th.

If you want to tell anything to Heaven, tell it to the wind.

—West African saying

STAR LEGACY

You, who have called
The Stars
And determined their number,
You also call each one
Of your people by name.
You know us from afar,
God both far and near.
You are the
Light of our eyes.

—Unknown

I dedicate this poem and this journal to Rochester who is my Star—and now this journal has come to its end.

Amen

The End of
Journal
(purple with Frogs)
March 13, 2000
to July 5, 2000

A journal follows after Meditations #2 and 3
(with only a few short entries omitted that are very personal)

JULY 28, 2000 TO MARCH 5, 2001

The Keeping and Care of Journals— now and forever

WRITER AND JOURNAL-KEEPER Rebecca Latimer, who wrote a delight-ful book, *You're Not Old Until You're Ninety—Best to Be Prepared However,* writes:

> I have been keeping journals ever since my childhood. My first notebook is dated 1914 and the latest is my present one. The bulk of them cover the twenty-five years I lived in Europe, the Middle East and Central America. They will end, I think, in California where I live now. These journals make a long uneven line on my shelf of the bookcase just across from my typewriter; they cover my entire life.

Imagine! I shared this quotation by Rebecca in my meditation on journal-keeping in my *Beside the Still Waters.* How I admire Rebecca faithfully keeping her journals since childhood. And like diarist and author Thomas Mallon that I wrote of earlier, she has overcome any fear of anyone else reading them by actually keeping them displayed on a bookshelf. You would find her book most unusual and inspiring. I wrote to her after reading her book for the first time and received a wonderful note back from her. She was now busy writing her autobiography at 93 years of age. See how vibrant and energetic writing can make you? Like myself, she is published by Blue Dolphin Publishing. Sometime after our exchange Rebecca passed away and I was very saddened to learn of her passing. She had revealed in her book that she intended leaving her journals to a library as encouragement to future generations to write and to keep journals. Because of Rebecca I plan to do the same, leaving mine to some far-off library in a distant state and no one I know shall ever know where. That is unless I succumb to an alternative plan in a moment of fear and first destroy them. Yes, I am allowing my private ones included in this book to be read as were small portions in previous books, but never was that ever my original intention. But oh--- there are other journals that I poured my heart into that can only be for myself alone. Perhaps every journal keeper has those but just does not speak of them. It is nothing to be ashamed of! Writing is a great healer. I can attest to that most emphatically! Journals let you pour your heart out and never scold or interrupt you.

Rebecca Latimer lived a number of years of her married life in our beautiful state of New Hampshire and then moved to California where we had begun our married life.

To write in a journal is a joy and it is also like having your own therapist in times that are difficult. I promise you that a journal is a faithful friend. Journal keeping is amazing. I do hope that you will try it if you never have or have not journaled in a long time. It is for your personal help and healing and your journal becomes your confidante.

Please try not to censor yourself. Fill your journal with not only writing from your heart but with all sorts of odds and ends, a running list of all the books you read (I do this!), quotes, (yes, always!) and anything that sparks your imagination like poems, (yes!—your own or of others) and even song lyrics that are meaningful. Unsent letters can also be written in your journal. If your heart is aching or you are in pain, write to the individual who wounded you if that be so, and vent yourself on your own journal pages. This brings a certain release and healing. There are no rules to journal keeping. None! So enjoy!

ONWARD

No matter what I do or say—
I am looked at in dismay.
It is as if it's carved in granite—
That I am from another planet.
But I am not so strange or odd—

Onward I just ever plod—
And on my journey try to do—
All that God would want me to.

Dedicated   Jan
to Rochester   August 2008

And I believe God has wanted me to write since I was a little child and it all began with diaries and journals.

MEDITATION THREE

Talking to Paper

Talking to paper is talking to the divine. It is talking to an ear that will understand even the most difficult things. Paper is infinitely patient.
—Burghild Nina Holzner, *A Walk Between Heaven and Earth: A Personal Journal on Writing and the Creative Process*

WRITING HELPS TO ELEVATE THE EMOTIONS to a level one can be more at peace. When I think I have forgotten certain feelings I can look back through entries in my journals and realize just how much I have grown, and too, where I still need work. The important thing to remember about journal writing is that the words should be spontaneous and from the heart. In the type journals I have kept I am talking to the paper, or perhaps consciously or subconsciously to another being either here on earth or in Heaven, and yet I am pouring myself out to the Divine. That can be different things to different persons. Writing will often promote healing and recovery as well as action or commitment yet most entries are concerned with every day problems, hopes, dreams, and hopefully joy. Many journals can be filled with sadness and grief and cries for help. How well I know this. You will gain more and more insight the more you write and when you are down or sad and depressed, if you read sections of your journals. You can then find that many times previously you have weathered difficult times and come through them. Your own words written in your journals can give you new strength to face new challenges in life. Think of your journal as a safe place, a Holy sanctuary. Know that your journal is for you alone and that no one can read what you have written without your permission. It is not necessary to write every day but writing as regularly as possible helps to preserve a

53

more rewarding record for yourself. You can see how you are changing if that is your wish, even though no one may ever tell you.

It is good to keep a notebook or small journal with you in the car. I may have mentioned that elsewhere but it is worth mentioning again. Or even if you are doing other things around the house or wherever you may be. When you have a helpful or interesting thought jot it down in that small book. Often important insights are lost when we fail to take the time to jot them down. As I have mentioned in previous books of mine and perhaps in this one, I have used steno pads for years and always have an on-going one near me. I now own piles and piles of completed ones. They are not my journals! Anything I put into this steno pad can then be transferred to my regular journal that I am using at the time if I wish to, but I keep that journal in a private place. I have covered so many aspects of journal writing in each of my previous books even though that was not the subject matter of each book. Journal writing is just so important! There are so many suggestions and ideas that would be helpful for you and some of my books were written in journal form after Rochester went to Heaven. There is a very long discussion on different journal types and interesting things related in my *Enchantment of Writing*. There are so many types of journals to buy, but also that you can create. Discussed in *Enchantment* are "Journals for Those Who Grieve" and "Journals for Your Family" and "Mother's Journals/Father's Journals" and "Photographic Journals." Also Anne Frank and her journal. This book you are reading now is the only type journal I wish to speak of now and that is the personal journal for you alone that you pour your most personal and intimate writing and thoughts into. Anne Frank's diary is of that nature also. I have written much about it in my *Enchantment* so I will just say very little here. You can refer to that book if you wish. As I wrote in there—how can one read about Anne Frank and not realize the importance and strength and beauty in writing. Look at other young teenagers you know between thirteen and fifteen years. Could they endure being locked in an attic for two years? Would they have something as incredibly valuable as Anne's writing to help and sustain them to live out this time? Would they turn to writing? We cannot answer but we pray it would be so. That she loved to write at such an early age before she had to be hidden away was her great asset. Does it not speak to hearts reading both this and her diaries to consider encouraging the joy of writing to young ones you know? Some never want to pick up a pen unless it is necessary for school and we have seen how computers are taking away the desire to write by hand. This is even noticeable in our own family with adults also. So please encourage the love of writing in a child when they are young.

I did with each one of my children and they never seemed disinterested and they all kept diaries or journals throughout their young lives though perhaps not faithfully. I still try to give them and their spouses each a new journal along with other gifts at Christmas. I know they encourage their children as do I with gifts of journals, and many write in journals. I also encouraged my own children to write letters—in many ways a form of journaling and discussed in *Enchantment*.

Anne's legacy to all is writing for it is life sustaining! I can attest to that! She never wrote about hatred anywhere in her diary but said she believed in the goodness of people. I believe through her writing great insights were given to her. I have had such blessings occur when I write. I have talked elsewhere about what we are given when we put pen to paper. Enough cannot be written about this young girl and yet I have personally known well three people in Pennsylvania declare she and her diary never existed nor did the holocaust. With words like these we can understand why there is such hatred in this world, but it did not exist for Anne.

Anne's diary was translated into fifty-five languages and more than 20 million copies have been sold. Films too have been made and many schools and streets all over the world have been named after this young girl. She has become a symbol of good news and courage. Can we not follow in her example of writing? If she cannot convince you of the importance of writing and journal-keeping, then I am not certain that I can. But oh, I am trying here for the sake of your souls, for writing will transform you. It will!

It is revealed that one thing you notice immediately about Anne's writing is her neatness. Anne wrote with her fountain pen in fine script page after page, hardly ever making a mistake or crossing out. I too have always tried to write very neatly and my rounded handwriting has not changed since I was a very young girl. Like myself, Anne had a beloved cat Moortje that had to remain behind when they fled their home. Anne wrote, "No one knows how often I think of her, Whenever I think of her I get tears in my eyes" (July 12, 1942). Along with all else, she had to leave her dear cat. How can it not be understood that writing is essential for the survival of the soul?

One of the first poems I wrote after meeting my wonderful friend (Dr.) Friar Francis and my return to writing poetry was this simple poem I wrote about my Blessed Mother Blue Parker pen that I used continually for years. ("Blessed Mother Blue" is a lovely pale blue.) After I became a vegetarian in 1989 I wrote only in green ink to signify nature and the environment and my love and protection of animals and I shall always use green ink. Pencils I use to write my manuscripts by hand as I am doing at this moment.

I share now—

ODE TO MY PEN

How faithful you stand
As I take you in hand—
You write on command
You meet my demand.

You know what I need
Incredible speed—
Free flowing ink
On call in a wink!

Ah, yes I salute you
With me forever—
I guard you as life
Loan you out?—Never!

Now others I know
Would not go to this end—
But God called me to write
And my pen is my friend.

This was my loving tribute to the pen who had been my friend. Please, always write. Make a pen your best friend.

Green and Violet Journal

$\mathcal{T}$HIS JOURNAL with its lovely green and violet cover (my favorite colors) with pretty water lilies on the front I began July 28, 2000. I misplaced it and it only has several entries in 2000 and some too personal to include here. A steadiness in recording entries begins February 18, 2001.

As in my other journals, pictures of dear cats are glued upon the upper right corners of the pages and photos of Rochester are here and there throughout—and other things I glued in I deemed worthy.

Inscriptions on inner first page. The first I later placed on a front page of my new book then—*Beneath the Stars and Trees—there is a place.*

Come with me to the enchanted forest. Trust the magic in the air, it is real. Take it with you wherever you go, for the magic you feel and want is ours if you simply believe.

—Melody Beattie, *Journey to the Heart*

*The realm of enchantment
is open to us all,
if we are willing to step
over the threshold.*

—Unknown

July 28, 2000

Today is the day I met Christ in 1992. I will never forget. It changed me. I am fully aware of Him every day. I talk to Him. His picture that

I drew is over my desk and a copy by my bed. I carry one also and put His picture in the front of all my journals. I am so thankful He came to me. No one can ever shake me on this. Today I asked Bob to make an appointment for Chester at the Vet's for his check-up. I know my Christ will be with Chester for a perfect check-up. I thank Him now in advance as I have been doing for several years.

OCTOBER 13, 2000

Announcing the birth of
Natalie Marie and
Melia Barbara Kolb
Born Friday, October 13, 2000
Natalie—nineteen and three quarter inches and six pounds, five ounces
Melia—twenty and a half inches and six pounds, 14 ounces
Born to George and Valerie
Big brother: Jameson Ronald
His second birthday October sixteen, 2000

Imagine! Twins!
And almost born on Jameson's birthday.
Thank you Jesus for helping Val and for the twins safe delivery.

God is crazy about you. If God had a refrigerator your picture would be on it. If He had a wallet, your photo would be in it. He sends you flowers every Spring and a sunrise every morning. Whenever you want to talk, He'll listen. He can live anywhere in the universe and He chose your heart. What about the Christmas gift He sent you in Bethlehem; not to mention that Friday at Calvary. Face it, He's crazy about you.

—sent to me by e-mail by my precious Jessica
after I got home from the hospital.

NOVEMBER 11, 2000

The following poem was sent to me by Cheryl, the lovely saleswoman and young mother who is also my sweet friend. We met in Bookland in Sanford, Maine where she worked and I visited every two weeks. She was responsible for placing my first two books in the Bookland stores.

She had copies of *Higher Ground* and *Compassion for all Creatures* everywhere in the store in displays. One entire window she filled with multiple copies of my books. It was such a gift. I could barely believe it. I would look in wonder at all the displays. In a card she gave to me this verse was within it.

For a long time
I've wanted to tell you
how much
it has meant to me—
having you
in my life.

(The poem has two more verses equally as lovely that I will not include in this book.)

She closed with her own written words

Thank you for all you are and all you do! I am very grateful and fortunate to have you in my life.

Love, Cheryl

And I too could write these very same words to Cheryl—and did write similar. She is a precious person and friend. We enjoyed talking about all the books we read and she shared her personal problems with me. All the while I browsed too, and selected books to buy and she waited on other customers when she was needed. It was in this store I had two Book-signings for my books arranged by Cheryl and at her suggestion. Blue Dolphin was very kind and made and sent many flyers for Bookland to advertise these signings ahead of time.

JANUARY 18, 2001

So much has happened since I last wrote in this journal. I have been looking all over for this journal and my turquoise "Rochester Chronicle" journal (the copy book). I lost it over the holidays—or I should say I lost *them*—and just found them an hour ago. I was so glad to get them back with me. I want to try and do better in my journal keeping. I have been using another journal but it is filled with so many sad entries of the past due to what happened in June of 1999, and filled with poems I wrote that are sad too, poems to help myself release my sadness, that I have not been sure I want to continue using it even though there are such wonderful things in there too. I may use both this and that one temporarily until I decide.

The "Rochester Chronicle" is mainly to do my "morning pages" in, but I put other things in it too plus I glue significant things in it mainly pertaining to my writing.

Anyway, I am glad I found these two journals and will keep them close by me now and hopefully I will write in them daily.

JANUARY 19, 2001—9:50 AM

I believe I have had a breakthrough in my writing for the book I began before Christmas. After some serious prayer yesterday which is written about in my other journal, I awoke this morning very early and could not sleep. When it was light I began to write. I have written many pages on "The Prayer of Poetry." It just flowed out and I again felt rejuvenated and like my writing had surfaced again after weeks of being suppressed by many things. Thank you Jesus for all that I wrote this morning. It just poured out. I have not read it as yet. Later today I will. We have to get ready now to go up to the Inn. Leslie and Stephen and a friend Brook have arrived at the Inn during the night as we expected them to—and we will go up there to be with them a little. Jess tells us after I just phoned, that they are still asleep. It is a dull day outside and snow is expected later. Every day is beautiful no matter what the weather.

11:05 AM

It is snowing and we have to leave for the Inn—but I just had to record an incident of answered prayer. This morning a brief e-mail came from Paul saying he has an idea for a cover for my *Enchantment of Writing* and to check the computer.

FEBRUARY 3, 2001

I have not written in here in so long and now have missed important things.

My breathing is incredible—so good it seems impossible, but I am too restless to write about that also but I thank my Christ with all my heart that I can go several days without using my inhaler. I will explain another time.

It is dusk now and Rochester is here with me as always. There are snow mobilers out on the lake. it reminds me of a poem we (Rochester and I) wrote about them years ago as I sat at my desk here on a Saturday night just as it is now—and Chester was sitting on our desk looking out the window then too—

> "Snow mobilers on the ice
> Circling once, circling twice."

That is how it began—but it was longer, of course.

Writing is a form of prayer.

—Franz Kafka

I will write in my other journal now too, because I cannot work on the book I began. It is time we go downstairs and we three begin our evening with dinner.

MONDAY, FEBRUARY 5, 2001

I have the statue in the photo on the previous page (there is a lovely photo glued in that I took) sitting on top of my manuscript *Beneath the Stars and Trees* to bless it and guard it. It has been in the middle of the kitchen table this way for weeks waiting until we hear from Paul. Please help the manuscript dear Christ and my Angels—and please help me. The statue was a gift from Bertha in September.

> *The woman who listens*
> *To her own quiet wisdom*
> *Creates harmony*
> *In her world.*

—Tao 45

TUESDAY, FEBRUARY 6, 2001

We had an amazing snow storm that began early afternoon yester-day and continued through the night. It is over 20 inches—more like 24 inches. We have already been ploughed. It is so beautiful outside, windy and cold, and I have taken a lot of pictures of the snow already. Rochester is here with me cuddled in his comforter asleep. Will pause to go to the Post Office now.

4:45 PM

Had a long and amazing letter from Joanne Clancy and part of it was about Rochester. There were other personal things in it too. Spiritual. I will write about it another time. It was about six typed pages long. It was really uplifting to me. I believe I know the interpretation about Roches-ter. It came to me immediately. It touches me so much.

The last two days I went to the Post Office forgetting to take my inhaler along! I am so free in my breathing and I do not even think of the inhaler. It is by the bed. For years it was always in my pocket even when I was in the house!

THURSDAY, FEBRUARY 8, 2001

Two more days without using my regular inhaler. I am totally free of it all day. It lies beside the bed. I do not keep it on me as I used to and do not take it to the Post Office. Acts of faith. It is a miracle! I feel wonderful and I believe I look healthier. Rochester says I do too.

I went to see Dr. Fleet yesterday to be checked in regard to the new inhalers. Will write about it later. It was all good!!! I continue to use them morning and before sleep at night—but use absolutely nothing in between. I feel free. I feel like I am totally healed. It is so exciting.

FRIDAY, FEBRUARY 9, 2001

I have written all about the inhaler in my other journal that is coming to completion now so I will not write about it here except to say every day is perfect and I do not ever need the inhaler during the day. It is still by the bed. I use only the other two morning and night and they stay by the bed too (Flovent and Serivent) Soon Dr. Fleet will remove one of them. I feel like a new person. I never have one breathing problem! I feel new!

Tomorrow Jessica, Renee and Clayton will meet Michael and Maxine in Boston after their two weeks in Russia! Jess cannot wait! We will be so happy to see them too!

This is the lovely Blue Dolphin that Barb gave to me for my birthday (a photo is glued in of it on this page) It is the sweetest thing and I keep it in my writing room near me. It is very special because she gave it to me and I named it "Delight." I called Barbie yesterday but she did not answer and I left a loving message on her machine. I still wear the two bead bracelets she made me all the time— and still have the ear cuff on my left ear with the pink heart on it she gave me. I have never taken it off since she put it on me. (Aside to reader—I still wear this same ear cuff all these years later—never removing it except for cleansing periodically. I get teased by Bob my ear will soon drop off—seven years later at this writing.)

Rochester is sleeping by me here on his soft quilt. He is so precious— my Angel.

> "I could not live life
> without my Rochester."

SATURDAY, FEBRUARY 10. 2001

What would happen if one
woman told the truth about
her life? The world would
split open.

—Muriel Rukeyser

9:25 AM

As I write Jessica is in Boston meeting Michael and Maxine right at this very time. I can only imagine how happy they all are.

Bob watched some games and I wrote and read and Rochester cuddled with me. So precious. We sold a brand new book that I had just given to Bob this morning to enter in our Enchanted Forest Bookshop. Fast!

> *Treating myself like a*
> *precious object will*
> *make me strong.*
> —Julia Cameron, *The Artist's Way*

This is the book I am reading now (a picture of it is glued in) that led me to record affirmations—but oh, so much more!!! (*Awakening Intuition* by Mona Lisa Schulz)

MONDAY, FEBRUARY 12, 2001

The little Angel Cat I glued on the previous page is one like an entire box filled with them that June gave me several years ago and I used completely. They were beautiful Angel Cats.

Meditation is to be aware of what is going on—in our bodies, our feelings, our minds and the world. Life is both dreadful and wonderful.

> *Don't think you have to be solemn to meditate.*
> *To meditate well, you have to smile a lot.*
> —Thich Nhat Hanh

The above quote I thought worthy enough to glue in here written by one of my favorite writers Thich Nhat Hanh—a most spiritual man and leader. His picture is by the quotation. I have written about him in my *Beneath the Stars and Trees* and I read his books regularly.

I will write more soon about things I have learned in regard to my experiences this past November and what the book *Awakening Intuition* by Mona Lisa Schulz revealed. It is amazing! I have written about it in great detail in another journal I just recently began in regard to those events, so I may not say too much in here. I am so grateful to have been led to the book that confirmed all I felt and knew intuitively!

There is a lovely poem entered here from a greeting card I sent Barbie. Though it is complete in my journal I cannot include but several lines here.

If I could
I would walk
through the night,
gently gathering up
all the most
beautiful dreams
in the world.

—Unknown

Too, I have pictures of Jessica and Barbie glued in on these pages, separately and together. So sweet—taken November 29, 2000 in our cottage and at the Inn.

SUNDAY, FEBRUARY 18, 2001

On Thursday, February 8, 2001 I began a journal and completed it on Saturday February 17, 2001. It is totally about the period of November 2nd through December 1st, the period when I first had discomfort in my chest area and extends to December 1st when Barbie left New Hampshire after being here with us two weeks. I had not been able to write anything about that period at all. But I am healed and different now and felt perhaps I should record all the details. Plus I had some confirming news through reading *Awakening Intuition* by Mona Lisa Schulz and that inspired me to write. I finished the journal in just over a week. It also contains many significant photos. I am pleased I was led to do it and that I followed through on it and completed it. I think it was a worthy thing to do. I think I will be glad I did it and when we are in our late, late 90s we can read it and find it interesting. It has a great deal about Barbie in it too.

On the opposite page here I will put the poem I wrote for her right after she left us and I will put it in the journal I just completed too. I wrote it on my Mother's birthday. This holds significance, plus in relation to the poem too, because Barbie was making jewelry and of course, that was my mother's work at Jewel Creaions—her store.

BARBARA

My daughter
      creates jewelry.
She threads minute beads
      onto elastic.
All are tiny seeds
      of love—sweet and fantastic—
            in various shapes and sizes.
Forming subtle patterns—
      with gentle surprises
            of color and form.
Each intricate beaded gift
      for me—
            made with her delicate hands—
Further lifts—and expands
      my already radiant heart anew,
            filled and spilling over
With love—so deep and true
      for her.
            She is my jewel!

Barbara Jan Egan
Nov. 2008

To my Barbie   Jan
with great love   December 3, 2000

Fact—Crickets have ears on their front legs just below their knees
that are extremely sensitive to sound vibrations.

TUESDAY, FEBRUARY 20, 2001

I am reading (from the library) Stephen King's latest book titled *On
Writing: A Memoir of the Craft* and thoroughly enjoying it. His language
is a bit rough at times (he swears on occasion but somehow it fits suitably
in his text) but his heart is so good and that is so evident and I really like
him as a person. I wish I could just sit and read it till I am finished but I
cannot. I began it late Sunday after finishing the other book I thoroughly
enjoyed and also from the library—*A Year By the Sea: Thoughts of an
Unfinished Woman* by Joan Anderson. When I finish Stephen King's I

will read the book pictured here on this page, a gift to me at Christmas from June *(Traveling Mercies* by Anne Lamott). Usually I buy all my own books but these three I did not. Very odd.

I will come back and discuss the books but I want to record that today is our George's 39th birthday and that seems utterly impossible. I just went over every detail with Bob of the day (or early morning) he was born.It seems like yesterday. And of course it was the day John Glenn orbited the earth though I could not watch this enormous event that day in the hospital for I had no television. Many others who had sons born in the hospital that day named them after this famous astronaut or gave parts of his name to their infants. I was told this by my physician Dr. Clayton T. Beecham. But we did not do that. We made one change however as we all know. George was to be "George Charles"—and after delivery and having a baby son after three beautiful little girls, I told Bob I wanted to change the name we selected to "George Robert—and this we did, the reason being obvious. And the "George" was for my Dad (his middle name) though there were other George's too on both sides of the family. It was a joyous day when our little George came to be ours. How we loved him! How we love him!

We called George at Brown University to wish him a wonderful day and he said he will call us back later to talk more. He will celebrate tonight at his home with Val and children and Janna, Bill and their children. It is wonderful they are all in Rhode Island and so close. George said they may be up here Thursday for the weekend.

It is interesting that yesterday I glued in this journal the poem I wrote for Barbie. I did not know that winging its way to me was a poem from Barbie that she wrote for me! And, had there been mail yesterday (there was not—Post Office was closed for President's Day!) I would have received her beautiful poem on the same day that I entered my poem for her in my journal. I do not know why I had never put it in any of my journals before. A true synchronism!

Poem sent to me : (Postmarked February 15, 2001)

> *Dear Mom*
> > *You're a wonderful girl—*
> > > *A genuine Pearl,*
> > *You're smart and clever—*
> > > *The sweetest Mom ever.*

> A Poet, A Writer
>> *You couldn't be Brighter.*
> I'm glad You're My Mother —
>> *Unlike any Other.*
>>> *I love you*

Barbara

I love Barbie, and this dear poem so much from her sweet heart. All the capitalizations are hers just as she wrote it all to me.

She wrote the poem on Blue Dolphin notepaper!! And she addressed it to:

Janny "Blue Dolphin" Kolb

The return address is:

Dianne Sawyer
Good Morning America
ABC
N.Y., New York

I love it!

She also told me on the envelope there was a little treat from Frankie and one from her, but Frank's treat was gone. Though she had the envelope well sealed and scotch taped, there was a slight slit in the side of the envelope and whatever was in it from Frank had gotten out the slit. It looked deliberate. There was a round imprint on the note card and envelope so it had been in there. Also the postage was extra—55 cents instead of 33 cents because of the enclosure. So the enclosure got out after it had been weighed and mailed. I feel so badly. I will have to tell them. I felt it might be a medal because of its round imprint. I just pray it was not an old one or a keepsake. I love that they sent such love. Barbie's poem is all love and it is so dear to me. I am so appreciative.

WEDNESDAY, FEBRUARY 21, 2001

Am debating whether or not to begin another journal exactly like the one I completed that holds all details and some photos regarding the month of November and my heart and its total health. I thought I had finished (the journal itself is finished) but now I see I wish I had room to include my conversations with Joanne (Clancy) who was praying for me and doing Reiki. Also she wrote me a very unusual letter recently and shared an incredible dream she had of Rochester in October and she wanted my interpretation of it. When I read the dream the first time it made me cry and I knew what I believe to be the interpretation of it. So I would like to have that in a journal too because it is about what happened to me in November.

Also after finishing Stephen King's memoir *On Writing* last night (read till 3 AM—I could not put it down) I feel I want to include something about that for a terrible incident in his life ties in with mine. So I will pray about all these things. I will write about Stephen King's book another time in more detail. It has really moved me. I did not want it to end. I am surprised at my reaction to it.

There is a tie-in also in regard to what we were both writing. We had both finished a book on writing. He actually titled his book that and mine was/is *The Enchantment of Writing*. I was proofreading mine as he was completing his after his terrible accident. I will write more about this. It is so unusual to me. He had this horrible thing happen to him physically the very same weekend I had the horrible thing happen to me emotionally! I will let it rest for now. I feel such empathy for him. He suffered so much and still is not right. At the time he was writing at the end of the book he was taking approximately 100 pills a day! I wish I could sit and talk to him. He is so unique and I believe he is a very good man. And I love how he loves and respects his wife and writes openly about it—and how she loves him! They met in college. Must close now. Of yes, and it is nice Stephen and his family live in Maine and not too far from here.

> *... is there anyone I sometimes wonder, who is not wounded and in the process of healing?—For me it is always poetry that comes as the healer—*
> —May Sarton, *Recovering: A Journal*

Yes, the writing and reading of poetry helps me so much too.

I forgot to mention that today was Uncle Frank Nagle's birthday and we love him. And the 19th was Uncle George Gray's birthday. And February 11th was Uncle Elmer McKay's birthday. All the Uncles' birthdays and each from a different line of the family—were all in February.

Tomorrow (22nd) is a significant day for me. Will mention it later. I called Barb today about her beautiful poem that she wrote and sent me but she was not there and I left a very loving message to her on the machine. I love her so much.

THURSDAY, FEBRUARY 22, 2001

No time to write except to say what an important day this has been to me through the years. I will just once again jot down the main reasons why but not the actual years.

1—February 22 (I will leave this one as a mystery. It was meant for my journal only)

2—February 22—(I went to Dr. D. Dalton Deeds in San Diego, in Balboa Park actually, and learned I was pregnant with my first baby.

3—February 22—Baby June Leslie and I met Bob in San Diego when his ship, the Piedmont, returned from overseas. He had been gone six months and missed June's birth and the first four months of her life. She and I had just flown in from Philadelphia the day before, where we had lived with my parents while Bob was overseas.

4—February 22—I received he Baptism of the Holy Spirit and also received my new "prayer language" (prayer "tongues" as written of in scripture).

5—February 22—Leslie June Hudson—our first granddaughter (and third grandchild) was born—the first daughter of our first daughter.

Thank you Jesus, for all of these blessings.

FEBRUARY 23, 2001

Today is Dad Kolb's 100th birthday. Both he and Uncle Elmer were 100 this month, Uncle Elmer on the 11th of February. Many live to be over 100. I wish they both had.

FEBRUARY 24, 2001

Val, George and children spent hours here today from noon till dinner time and I made vegetarian lasagna and (veggie) chicky pats while they were here. Later George went over to the Birchgrove with Bob to see what was going on over there and ended up taking seven of our books from our on-line bookstore he was interested in. It was a great day and Rob called shortly before they left not knowing they were here. He had not talked to us in a long time and wanted to connect. We had a good time talking as Rob and I always do and it meant very much that he called. Talked to June briefly too.

I am rereading Stephen King's book *On Writing*. It is supposed to snow again in the morning and quite a lot. I hope we will be able to get out to go to church. The car is parked at the top of the hill at Dennis's in case of the storm.

Chester is here asleep on my legs as he was earlier in the living room. So dear. My precious little one.

Help me dear Christ, to get back to my writing. I have not been able to work on my book these last few days with wonderful family here. Thank you.

SUNDAY, FEBRUARY 25, 2001

It began to snow as predicted before we left for church and as we awoke. But I still wanted to go and not be held back while we could still get out. We always do that. If we wake and it has snowed all night, then it is harder to get out or not at all till the plough comes. With the new Pathfinder (new to us—but not new) we get out when we could not before—and all the bigger snowfalls seem to have been on week days. We have not missed any church.

Went to Mass and then picked up a couple of items at Shop 'N Save plus the Sunday paper and went directly to the Inn. We spent till early evening there with George, Val and children and of course Michael, Jessica Maxine, Renee and Clayton. It was great! We were in the kitchen the entire time and Bob and I were holding the babies the entire time. Isabelle and Critter were there too, of course. So sweet.

It was still snowing when we left to come home. Renee called to see if we got home safely and we called to see if George and Val did in Rhode Island, but had to leave a message on their machine. They did not answer.

We had not been ploughed when we got home. It was so good to see Rochester who was waiting inside the door after serenading us by his walk on the piano keys. We spent all evening together cuddled and it is so hard to have to leave him when I absolutely have to go out—but I know he is safe and fed and gently waits our return.

Dreams are the quickest way into our inner world.
They astonish us with their wisdom about past, present and future.

I do not know who said that. Dreams are on my mind and heart right now. I have mysterious and lovely quotes about them in my Commonplace Book but do not know their sources. Some are from myself.

A dream can often tell us what and where a problem is
long before a doctor can diagnose.

I realize that now much more since my own experience in 2000.

The dream arises from the instinctual world.

Yes, I know this

If the dream uses a symbol and you say, "That's bizarre! Chuck it,"
you're chucking gold.

I know in my own experience that it is difficult to know exactly what a symbol means in a dream. Sometimes I do immediately understand if I am able to capture it and then write it down, but the symbol can be for so many parts of myself like the imagination or mind or heart and sometimes we have to wait. Years later we may only then begin to understand.

I know too if we are filled with anger or rage we have to eventually express it in some way and get it out of us or it can take other forms—particularly illness. When I experienced all that I did that crushed and hurt me beyond words in 1999, I began writing *Beneath the Stars and Trees.* I wrote about everything I could think of and describe about living in this beautiful woods by a lake so I could help to heal myself of the horrible brokenness and humiliation that was put on me. Christ was there with Rochester as I wrote. Rochester is my inspiration and is ever faithful and there with me—a visible sign of God. Please, dear Christ, may I soon know that *Beneath the Stars and Trees* is accepted. I place my trust in You. Thank you, dear Christ. Amen!

I have not gotten all my thoughts together yet in regard to Lent but I do have a couple in mind. When I get them firmed up I will enter them in here.

It was an Ash Wednesday in February 1977 that I sat in Nazareth Hospital in Philadelphia with my mother after kissing my dad goodbye up in his room before he was taken on the litter to the operating room. He was having his larynx removed. It makes me sick to think of it. It took so long. I will never forget what it was like when I saw him afterwards. He had been so sweet when we said goodbye while he was on the litter. It was the last time I heard his normal voice—there in the hall before his operation. I will wait to write more later—if I do at all. It gets me so upset and so sad inside.

2:30

Extra! Extra! I asked Bob if we have any Stephen King books in our bookshop for sale and he said we had one and brought it over just now. It is *The Green Mile*—made into a movie with Tom Hanks on the cover. I am so excited. I want to read it! I know the movie was said to be very good and the book at first came out in supplements with different covers than the one I have. That is because the movie had been released and they used the cover I guess, to connect with and promote the movie and vice versa. There is a different photo of Stephen King in the back than is in his book *On Writing*. All his books are listed in the front of this one so I will enjoy looking at it more carefully later. I cannot allow myself to do that now or I will not get any writing done.

Am cooking some short grained brown rice in the oven for the first day of Lent. If it turns out, I have not cooked any in months, I want to try putting some in Chester's food too. We will see.

5:15 PM

Had a tiny bowl of the brown rice after going to the Post Office and it was delicious! We will have it for dinner—all three of us! I looked over *The Green Mile* while having the brown rice with tea when we came back from the Post Office and I am anxious now to read it. I wrote a long letter on some of the new stationery Bob made me to Barbie and Frank thanking them for the three gifts I received yesterday.

They are so sweet. I will write about the gifts soon.

Fairy and Unicorn

I love this mystical picture (glued in above this journal entry) and have glued it in past journals too. It was in the Sunday paper and I cut it out. Magical!

> *If I did not*
> *have you as my*
> *Mother*
> *I would choose*
> *you as my*
> *Friend*

The beautiful verse above is in a small plastic encased key ring holder. It has a pastel flower design in the background of it. On the reverse side is a sweet picture of Barbara with a precious smile. Barbie is beautiful. Frank apparently put the things in the plastic and the note says he did it but it is from her. I wish I could wear it. I am so appreciative.

Also there was a sweet Blue Dolphin puppet (hand type). So cute! I was using it to show Chester and he would sniff its nose. It is a cute puppet and Barb has been attentive in giving me Blue Dolphin things which began when she was here. She bought me a beautiful Blue Dolphin music box too. It was not for an occasion but a love gift. And it means so much. There have been other Blue Dolphin gifts and now this sweet puppet. Also a silver anklet with dolphins. Each and every surprise so significant to me.,

We had the brown rice for dinner that I made this afternoon and it was delicious to us all. I put mushroom sauce on it but when I first tried it after it finished cooking I ate it plain and it was great. I did not put a sauce on Rochester's portion.

Chester was with me all evening on my legs as he is now. He is so beautiful and loving, so gentle and dear. Priceless.

FRIDAY EVENING, MARCH 2, 2001

I just want to enter now some amazing news! My latest book, *Beneath the Stars and Trees—there is a place*, is accepted for publication. It is accepted! Paul and Bob talked from 1 to 2 PM and it is accepted! I am overjoyed! Thank you, thank you, dear Christ. Thank you, dear Chester.

There have been times when for me the act of writing has been a little act of faith, a spit in the eye of despair.

—Stephen King

And I say "yes, yes" to that. He goes on to say that *"writing is not life, but I think that sometimes it can be a way back to life."*

It has surely been that way for me. And he adds that it was something he found out in the summer of 1999 when a man driving a blue van almost killed him—and I add it was a black and white van that almost killed me. This horrendous van almost took his physical life and the van in my life struck me in the deepest core of my emotions. I thank God Stephen King survived.

SATURDAY, MARCH 3, 2001

I am still in an aura—still caught in the moment of hearing that my book *Beneath the Stars and Trees—there is a place* has been accepted by Paul at Blue Dolphin. Oh, thank you, dear Christ, thank you, dear Mary. You know how my heart and soul is in this book. You know! You were there through it all as was my sweet Chester.

I will have to begin a new journal soon. I have enjoyed this one and have gotten back in the swing of writing daily —or almost. Also finished another journal recently that had been on-going that has a lot of the past pain in it. Plus, I finished the special journal I wrote in about the events of November that I completed in a week and a day. So I am doing better in journal writing and that should help now in the writing of my book. I do not want to discuss that now.

I had an e-mail from Paul today that Bob believes has a special message for me after their talk yesterday and the acceptance of my book. His wife had received it and Paul sent it to us. It had been placed on the windshield of a woman's car, the one who sent it to Nancy Clemens.

It reads:

> *Good morning! This is God.*
> *I will be handling all your problems today.*
> *I will not need your help.*
> *So relax and have a great day!*

I feel like God is speaking directly to me through this. Thank you, God.

Sunday, 2:15 am, March 4, 2001

Am nearing completion on the second reading of *On Writing* by Stephen King.

Monday, 5:10 pm, March 5, 2001

A cute photo on the opposite page I took of my beloved Rochester sitting on the books I ordered (the book that touched me so deeply) to share with others. I am sure I have written about *A Change of Heart* in this journal and I ordered these extra copies to share with others. Rochester both laid on the pile or sat on the pile while it was on the end of the table for several days. He knows how this book amazed and touched me. He was there as I read. He blessed the books with his presence upon them. He knows things of the heart. It is true. He laid upon me to help me. He always lies on me. He always helps me.

It has been snowing all day and they say it is going to be a whopper here and all up the coast from Pennsylvania on, but it does not seem out of the ordinary so far. We will see.

I cannot get Stephen King's book out of my mind and his accident. I finished it yesterday for the second time and I will buy it and own it. It is one of those books like Thomas Moore's *The Re-enchantment of Everyday Life* that I will keep going back to again and again. I have read T. Moore's book five times and quoted often from it in several of my own books and I know I will read it other times. I hope Bob will read tonight the portion about Stephen's accident. He remembers as do I when it was all over our local news and all news programs.

I am thanking God continuously for answered prayer that my book *Beneath the Stars and Trees* is accepted by Blue Dolphin! Received mail today about Dolphins and that seemed another touch of confirmation. This picture is from the envelope (glued in above writing).

I have to begin another new journal soon. I have been so faithful in writing as I explained earlier that I do not want to break the habit. It is so good for me! I have so many pretty journals waiting to be used it will be hard to select one. And I have so many journals written in and completed! I have truly enjoyed this pretty one and love the water lilies that are like the ones out on our lake in summer. The cover is so soft and appealing in my two favorite colors of green and violet. The back cover is violet alone with swirls through and the front cover has the lilies with a touch of the violet on the edge. The inside covers front and back, are like the front cover of green and violet in the art work except they are all soft violet and no green.

On the opposite page for fun is an older photo we found recently and Bob made some copies for me. I sent a larger one to George in a card and plan to send one to Bob (Gottlieb). The three of them, Bob (G), Bob (Kolb) and George are acting like the Lollypop kids from the *Wizard of Oz* with their hats (all had received them for Christmas. Stockings hung on mantle are in the background), Bob's leg bent funny and Bob (Kolb's) mouth is funny too trying to look like a Lollypop kid but this picture is too small to see it. George is such a young boy in the picture (but as tall as his dad) and Bob G. had long hair. So many years have passed.

LATER

Writing is magic, as much of the water of life as any other creative art. The water is free. So drink. Drink and be filled up.

—Stephen King

TUESDAY, 1:06 AM, MARCH 6, 2001

There was such upsetting news on tonight about Vice President Dick Cheney. It really distressed me. I have been praying for him since November. Dick Cheney has a history of heart attacks that go back to 1978. God bless him. He admitted himself to the hospital yesterday because of chest discomfort at two different times and he had other procedures done—new ones. He did not have a heart attack this time and will go home today and is expected to go back to work Wednesday. He said when interviewed, he had not been eating properly. He eats meat and chicken still and probably feels like he has to in his position, but his life is more important. He said he is doing better now in regard to eating. Please dear Christ, take care of Dick Cheney and do not let him have another heart incident. Please! I sound like a strong Republican but I am not. I just feel sorry for him. Perhaps I will send him a card because of this incident—a card of encouragement. He may never get it but I will still try to do it and hope the Angels make sure he gets it.

It is still snowing out and all up and down the coast it is setting records. I guess we will be snowed in tomorrow. We had three book orders today we were able to mail out. That was great!

Got some writing done on my latest book I am working on—about prayer. Thank you, Jesus, that our (Rochester's and mine) *Beneath the Stars and Trees* is accepted!!!

TUESDAY, 1:30 PM

If you don't know where you are, then you don't know who you are.
—Wendell Berry

Animals may aid us in our everyday lives, in our dreams, meditations. Since they were created before humans, they are close to the Source and can act as allies, guides and familiars in our search for wholeness.
—an Inuit Woman

The snow is amazing and so deep. Continues to fall and blow too. Talked to Jess, and the girls have a snow day here in New Hampshire and Michael is home from work. Center Ossipee is getting the snow just as we are in East Wakefield. I made oatmeal and a baked potato (small) for Bob and me for breakfast again—which was really brunch (after 12 PM) We do not always like to eat earlier and did some work first before eating. Am going to begin work on my book now. I had some new ideas come to me about it last night that I wrote down. My beloved little Rochester is here with me on his wildlife quilt ready to assist me and sometimes nap. I even pick up his precious thoughts then too. It is a glorious day and we are together.

I cannot end this journal without writing an unusual incident which I think I failed to record. In years to come it will amaze me and make me laugh but at the time it did not. On Thursday (I think) February 15th, Bob and I started out for Sanford. (It was the day I got Stephen King's book from the library.) We had had an ice storm the previous day. Everything looked beautiful, snow, trees etc.—but our hill was a sheet of ice! I started out the side porch door and was only able to get a few feet up the hill and realized I could not go up or down—it was so dangerous! I had slipped many times and at last had found one safe spot. It was upsetting and Bob was kind of laughing at me, but I was desperate. I could not move! Finally I just got down on my hands and knees and crawled all the way up our big hill (all 150 feet of it) to our car that was parked in front of Dennis's cottage! That is a long way to crawl. I kept throwing my pocket book out ahead of me and then catching up with it. Bob did it finally on foot, but had fallen down twice and rolled to the bottom of the hill. It is not something I would like to do again but it was an accomplishment.

And so I end this journal that has many significant things in it for me, and shall begin another.

THE END (NO, NOT QUITE)

No, I see it is not the end! The pages were stuck together. I will stop now though and add something later.

I actually have completed this journal rather quickly no matter what the dates on the bookplate in front say. Most of the journal has been written rather faithfully just since January 18th (2001) in less than two months. I will try to be faithful in my next one.

Tonight I saw Lama Suyra Das, author of a book I own *Awakening to the Sacred: Creating a Spiritual Life from Scratch*. I was impressed and he was very spiritual and gentle and his remarks were inspiring. He also expressed his love for animals and his own dog, and told of the Buddhist belief that animals are to be treated as humans and that they have souls. I had written so many similar things in my *Compassion for All Creatures*. I am pleased I was able to see and hear him and will certainly buy another of his books. I like the one I own and quoted from it in my own book that I wrote.

This then is the end of this journal and it too has a holiness within it. Too, because Rochester has been continually with me through the writing of every page.

THE END

From the time he was a kitten, Rochester always loved books and journals.
1986

Journaling Through Grief and All Seasons of the Soul

Like no other tool, the diary helps to explore our feelings,
our private struggles, as well as our peak experiences.
Ah, how rewarding to be alone for a reflective moment!
And how well this solitude can be used for that journey inward—
—Curtis W. Casewit, The Diary: A Complete Guide
to Journal Writing

THE MORE YOU JOURNAL the more at ease you will be with the discipline or process of putting words on paper. You have infinite worth as a child of God. Your very own words, even your descriptions of what may seem to be very ordinary things to you, are truly important and unique. You may be surprised at your expanding creativity. Truly journaling unlocks the imagination and a certain freedom begins to come. Your journal will become such a friend that will know more about you and your inner life than any person may ever come to know, except someone or someones extremely close. Your journal may be one of the first possessions after your personal loved ones, human and animal, to be saved in case of fire or flood.

Though I kept many journals throughout my life that covered all aspects of emotions, the writing of my *In Corridors of Eternal Time* helped me spiritually and emotionally more than any others. I was in the deepest grief I had ever experienced and when I put pencil to paper writing day by day on this journal manuscript I felt the oneness with Rochester and his guidance in ways so intense that I could never doubt all I knew to now be true. All my deepest beliefs were radiating within and around me in the fullness of his continual presence. It has been so since 2002 when he passed. Writing *Solace of Solitude*, the journal that followed, was also a similar emotional experience.

I am always in the present moment. I know I have said that more than once in this manuscript and in my other books, but it is truth and strength. Thich Nhat Hanh often refers to the *suchness of the moment*—the form of this only moment there is. I lose track of the years since 2002 and there is *only the present*. I am amazed when an incident or memory surfaces to discover it happened in 2003 or 2006 when to me it is alive *as if in this very moment*. I feel I have been shown the most blessed way to live if I stay in the present moment. I truly have been shown it gives me a timelessness and a peace of heart even though I shall always grieve.

The first verse of a lovely old poem that has become such a treasure to me since 2002 reads —

> *I shall not make a garment of my grief,*
> *Enshrouding me, for all the world to see;*
> *But I shall wear grief as a secret charm,*
> *Where none may see—close to the heart of me.*

The poet goes on to write in the third stanza that those who grieve shall know the charm is there—close to the heart—and they will smile and understand as only the grieving can. I actually carry Rochester's Anima within my soul.

My spiritual friend John Edward and spiritual helper and comforter to countless others has said many times, *"You never get over the loss of a loved one—you get through it,"* and I believe the secret is to live in the moment. Though I tried to do this long before 2002, it seems that since 2002 I have succeeded and live in this timelessness, and it is truly other-worldly how one lives and moves and has their being as a result. And those loved ones close to me who have passed away really are close to me. They are very much now in the present and to be experienced in love.

Because of this new closeness and presence my dad especially has become exceptionally present to me though he passed away much too early 31 years ago. As a result I was led to write a book about him last year for the 30th anniversary of his passing that will soon be published titled *Silent Keepers—Ellis and Rochester.* This timelessness I experience in the present moment allowed me to write an entire book when I did not think I could write more than a few pages because of my lack of knowledge about his life.

There is an awesomeness and sacredness of other dimensions with me continually, for too, I carry Rochester's Anima within me forever— his *"breath, soul"* that entered me the moment he went to Heaven as I held him. For when that word Anima entered my mind I instantly knew what to do even though in my aching grief I did not even know my own name. It can be read about in detail in my *Corridors,* for there is a sacredness in that book of Rochester's and mine and it is meant to be read in detail within *those very pages* and not in these. It is entered forever in a journal of my own handwriting and then in his published *Corridors* so that it might help others who grieve. While I was writing this book you are reading now, I received an e-mail from a man who lives in another part of New Hampshire, a stranger. He was deeply grieving for his dear little cat had recently entered Heaven. He told me how much *Corridors* was helping him and that he had chosen it on-line to purchase over other books there on grief. I feel Rochester's loving spirit drew him to our book so that he might receive help. We exchanged several e-mails and now he is on his journey as I am on mine. I spoke too of the importance of keeping a journal and through the writing of my journal *Corridors* I personally have been helped immensely as I know this man has also, and I pray others are too. Writing is so essential to your passage through life. It is necessary for this journey!

When you act *as if* you are receiving strength and help you *will* receive it especially when you attempt to give this.

Often I needed help so badly after Rochester passed—and too, earlier in 1977 and 1978 when my parents and uncle went to Heaven and in the years that followed, but it was very rarely there. In my writing of my books I helped myself and hopefully others, and in the writing of my journals. I acted *as if* I could travel this passage, and I am. And I pray always. Faithfully! And I meditate.

I felt now God wanted me to learn these insights and strengths on my own and to live out what I was learning. The aloneness, like the present moment, is a strength. It is written:

The deeper the sorrow, the less tongue it hath.

—The Talmud

May Sarton is a writer who has been part of my writing life since I was introduced to her through her *Journal of a Solitude*. A writer of many published journals, poetry and novels who lived long in New Hampshire and then in York, Maine, before her passing wrote about her cat Scrabble after having to have her put to sleep.

I was crying so much. I felt cracked in two. In some ways the death of an animal is worse than the death of a person. Partly it is absolutely inward and private, the relation between oneself and an animal and also there is total dependency.

Like myself she was overwhelmed in grief writing: "I kept thinking as I drove home, this is all inside me, this grief. I can't explain it, nor do I want to, to anyone." In your grief or weakness you will receive strength and help when you live as if you are already receiving it. It just happens! My spiritual friend Martin Scot Kosins, author of Maya's First Rose, also feels this unending grief for his dog Maya. Later May Sarton wrote in her journal—

I wish for your rare purrs and for your sweet soft head butting against my arm to be caressed.

—*The House by the Sea*

The term "as if" I had known for years in my spiritual life but it became so very important and utterly necessary in grief. But it is a part of all of living especially when living in the present moment or in the Sacrament of the Moment as it is written of in the Christian faith—for when you live *as if*, you are.

Journal about this until it is becoming a part of you and it is ingrained within you. You then can read your very own written words for strength.

This author is speaking of the death of her daughter Paula when she writes:

I don't want to get rid of that sadness, it's part of who I am today. I feel like its a fertile soil at the bottom of my heart where everything wonderful grows—creativity, compassion, love and even joy.
—Isabelle Allende, interview in *Writer's Digest*

This well known writer adds to her words that she has the joy of knowing that there is a spirit she can connect to. She has written two books about her daughter Paula years apart. In 1992 she wrote a memoir following her passing and now she has written a series of letters to her. I do this often to Rochester in my journals.

One thing I have always done since I become a resident of New Hampshire and even long before moving here permanently, is to wave to strangers, be they walking along the road (there are no sidewalks in our rural areas) or driving. That does not mean I wave to every car or person for that is not possible—but I know when the opportunity is present and act upon it. I wave *as if* in greeting and acknowledgment! And especially in grief you cannot know what comes back into you whether the individual waves back to you or not. When you give, something is given back to you as you are told in scripture. There is a certain joy and child-like gift that you have given. And it is good for the soul at any time but especially in sadness. This little wave is a lovely little New Hampshire trait I learned here and I am glad for it. (I often do it when we go to Maine too. Folk there are friendly and receptive too.) It never fails to lighten when I take the present moment to do it and also when I receive a wave first or in return of my own. In my experience it was not done in Pennsylvania or other states, but it is lovely to do all over the United States, all over the world, everywhere we are. Then journal about it. Use every opportunity to write in your journal and to record your present moments. You are creating a treasure book for yourself—like a little spiritual medicine chest for the soul. Always write!

... we will understand that our grief is now a part of who we are. Like the memory of our loved ones, grief will never disappear, we just grow stronger to support the weight of it.
—George Anderson, *Walking in the Garden of Souls*

And writing in a journal will give you a strength you cannot expect or imagine until you begin this discipline. Always write!

President Ronald Reagan wrote in his private journal every night at his desk after a full day of official duties. They were large journals he kept and we learned more about this fine man and his discipline of journal writing from his wife Nancy when interviewed by Larry King about two years ago. (But then it could have been two weeks ago. I live in the present moment.) Five of his journals she had published and the one original she showed that night like the other four, was large, thick and leather bound! Those five journals represent hours, nights and years of writing! At times he wrote so child-like of personal things it was tender. When he was shot and almost died, he simply wrote, "It hurt." Other matters concerned his daily life as President. If the head of our country valued the act of journal-keeping perhaps his discipline will speak to your heart more than mine. It has nothing to do with politics—his, mine, or yours, but everything to do with the soul.

Also may his spirituality be a light to others for he wrote that he had to forgive the man that shot him and who nearly took his life or he could not expect God to forgive him. This simple but profound statement is now known through his once very exclusively private, but now published journals that he quietly sat alone and wrote in every night as a release and solace. How can we ever disregard or minimize the importance of keeping a journal. To nightly write in his journal alone in the oval office was the last act he did before allowing himself to enter his personal life. His journal, in a sense, was like a connecting living bridge.

Another well known journal keeper and writer that has influenced me for good writes:

As for style of writing, if one has anything to say, it drops from him simply and directly, as a stone falls to the ground.
—Henry David Thoreau (1817–1862)

I have a gentle feeling that President Reagan, a journal keeper like myself and a deeply spiritual man and his Nancy, might too have been blessed at close of day by a prayer we say nightly. It is a new prayer that Bob wrote for us several years ago adapted from an old prayer we said as children. I have included it in each of my books except the first, and it is handwritten in many of my journals. This prayer was in addition to our own silent prayers at night and my blessing Rochester's forehead with the Sign of the Cross. I still give Rochester this gentle blessing in spirit. Perhaps you may wish to pray this prayer also from time to time, or enter it in your journal. It is assuring and childlike.

> *As I lay down to sleep this night*
> *Please keep me safe 'til morning light.*
> *Grant me sleep and needed rest*
> *And fill my dreams with happiness.*
> *For Lord I know that with you near*
> *There's nothing that I have to fear.*
> *Guide me where you want to lead*
> *And be with those I love and need.*

Before Rochester passed, Bob had also written music for the prayer and recorded it on his electronic keyboard on a separate tape. It is beautiful.

Before settling down for prayer and sleep upon my legs, Rochester often climbed gently up the front of me as I sat in a half-reclining position and he would push his little forehead against mine numerous times, a form of a kiss. Often he would gently pat my cheek with his soft white marshmallow paw, a tender touch of his love—not only at night but often in our writing room when he was on my lap or desk. Thus this poem was written for him on his birthday May 30, 1995 with great love and in gratitude.

SOUL'S TOKEN

"My kitten's tender paw, thou soft, small treasure"—*
Upon my cheek or hand—brings joy unspeakable, and pleasure
That cannot be written—nor spoken.
It is his giving of love, his token
From his soul—expressed in merest touch.
And I receive—and love him, oh so very much.

Jan
June 7, 1995

*Quote by Heinrich Heine (German Poet)

Spiral Notebook Journal

(With drawing of a little marmalade cat on the cover
symbolic of Rochester)

MAY 7, 1993

*L*ast night I dreamed many dreams but only fragments can I re-member. This has been true every night I have been here —many dreams but not retention of them—only little bits and pieces. But last night (or really early this morning) I dreamed a dream very unusual

—very brief but disturbing. I dreamed I was in a darkened room and suddenly my mother was standing right in front before me and though the light was so dim, I definitely could see and tell it was my mother without having any proof. She stood there so close to me. It was startling to me and she seemed downcast in expression though it was hidden in the dark. Yet I knew her head was bent down. I suddenly felt sorry for her. I threw my arms around her neck and said, "I love you, Mother," and I could see my own face looking over my arm from a vantage point of behind my mother. It was like I was there in the dream hugging her neck but also seeing myself doing it from behind my mother. In the background vaguely I sensed a man walking or taking a step across the room and it seemed to be the profile of my father when he was younger. That was the end of the dream. It was very strange because I cannot remember when I last had a dream about my mother, or I am not certain that I have although I have of my father. I am fairly sure I must have dreamed of my mother but I cannot remember it now although if I did I am sure it will be recorded in my journal. I do not know what the dream meant or what she was trying to say. She seemed sad. She was not clothed in the dream but this was obscured from me by the darkness in the room. I could never see her in that way. She was very modest in life and her nakedness always obscured then. She kept me in the dark then—so to speak and that is lovely. I am like she is in that way and modest too. I could only think that perhaps it represented that she was in Heaven (and of that I am certain) and clothed in a new way and that I no longer could see her in clothes that people wore on earth—therefore she was unclothed because I could not see her heavenly garments either. I only know there was a specific reason for her being unclothed because that was not my mother's nature or to expose her body in that way or provocative ways. I can only pray more interpretation will be given eventually because it was a most puzzling dream and I want to learn more about it. It was quite vividly with me when I woke. That I retained it so exactly and clearly to write it down means so much to me.

Postscript—In the second sentence of this journal entry I write "this has been true every night I have been here." At that time in our lives we still lived in Pennsylvania but made frequent extended trips to our cottage here in New Hampshire until we moved here permanently in January 1996. This dream took place in New Hampshire as did all the hypnogogic images that follow. Too, this was the only thing recorded in this journal in 1993. All else was recorded in 1995, begun anew February 18th.

MARCH 23, 1995

After meditation in twilight imagery I saw a series of white angels one at a time. Then I saw so clearly a young man in brown pants and suspenders with white shirt sleeves rolled up and a hat on the back of his head (the kind with brim all way around—not a cap) running to jump onto the back of a truck that had steps going up the back flat against the back of the truck. He ran and made it and jumped on clinging to the rungs of the ladder or steps and rode off on the back. It ended. It was like a Norman Rockwell painting. What does it mean? It was all so clear it was like seeing a movie.

APRIL 9, 1995

In twilight imagery today following meditation I saw clearly a light car. Then I saw a girl with long dark hair running to her car in a parking lot and unlocking it and driving away. I then saw a girl kneeling in front of two grave stones—one stone in front of the other. I think it was the same girl—her back to me but her hair was long. The other girl had jeans and blouse on. I cannot say about the one kneeling. Then I saw a single grave stone with no one there.

I also saw a little mouse like the one Bob catches in his humane tender traps run under the table in the living room—the table next to Bob's chair. The mouse ran into the front area of the table.

This was followed by three or four white angels in different poses. They appeared out of a burst of white light—all in the same way. (many did before in other meditations—appear in a burst of light, but not all) They came one after the other not all at once. I saw a white animal again—either a horse or unicorn. It came and left too quickly

APRIL 22, 1995

Following a long meditation period today—a very deep one—I received a clear image of two large white unicorns in the lower portion of what was like a picture and the rest was green and outdoors. The unicorns were side by side and seemed more like lovely fanciful drawings of unicorns rather than real unicorns. I do not think it was twilight imagery or Hypnogogic Imagery but rather seemed to be part of my meditation. I should not have begun this entry with the word "following" because I feel now the unicorns were in the meditation itself near the end.

Why do I see unicorns so often—unicorns and angels—always white? Such a blessing. It must mean something very wonderful and I hope I will soon know. The unicorn has become meaningful to me this past year or more and I have entered things in here about that. These were large unicorns together. Before I saw each unicorn alone and it was smaller each time in comparison with these today and very real looking.

APRIL 23, 1995

I had such deep and long meditation periods today. I was troubled and sad and had been crying frequently over the bombing in Oklahoma City and the loss of the dear people and for the loved ones who lost them and perhaps that is why the meditations were so deep. I saw a white animal quickly in Hypnogogic Imagery but it was so fast I could not determine what animal it was.

I also saw at separate times what appeared to be white heads or skulls and yet not quite in bony skeletal form but cavernous so that light was within them shining out the eyes and other openings. It was not really frightening and yet strange. I wonder now if it could relate to the deaths in Oklahoma City. Could the light mean the light within these individuals that died was shining forth out of them—that they give light to those left behind? That is the first and only thing that has come to mind. I have been so sad today. Bob and I have had on-going spiritual discussions and I am without answers for myself and those poor people in Oklahoma who have died—and those who have remained to live and mourn their dead loved ones. I have so many thoughts and questions. I feel like I want to write them all down yet do not have the energy to do it because it all wore me down today just the conversations and thoughts and then seeing the TV at 4 PM when the great Ecumenical Prayer Service came on for all the people in Oklahoma, and President and Mrs. Clinton were there and Billy Graham and others. Bill Clinton's words were marvelous and sensitive and healing, and Billy Graham's were also. I have so much sorrow in me. This is all so horrible.

LATER

This poem in its first form was going around inside me following my meditation period and writing. Several hours later while seeing more news on TV from Oklahoma I made several revisions in the poem and I think it is as it is supposed to be now.

No, I just was given the word "Justice"— for no one can have peace or a new lease on life after this tragedy unless there has been justice as President Clinton promised. I will write it out again.

FOR OKLAHOMA CITY

A bomb has blown up all those lives!
It is as if thousands of knives—
Have been plunged into the hearts of the living—
Those who keep sorrowful watch—giving
Forth of their love and tears
Their hopes and fears—
For all those in this tomb of pain.
Out of these twisted ruins and ashes
May there arise answers—and flashes
Of wisdom—and insights and justice and peace—
That will fill hearts and souls and minds with a new lease
On life,—so that the dead may not have died in vain.

Jan
April 23, 1995

APRIL 24, 1995

In meditation saw two white snow flakes each totally different and at separate times in Hypnogogic Imagery. They each began small and grew larger then disappeared. Each extremely white. What does it all mean?

LATER

Had a meditation and saw many white Angels but all separately and all very different sizes and types bursting into being then disappearing. All lovely.
(in Hypnogogic Imagery)

APRIL 28, 1995

Had a long meditation today quite deep and near the end a small white Angel came in Hypnogogic Imagery and a small white house.

APRIL 29, 1995

A small slender white figure—angelic-like sitting then standing with one foot on rocks. An adult figure—but just small in size in my imagery.
(Hypnogogic Imagery following meditation)

MAY 3, 1995

I had meditation this morning but I was upset over something that had just happened. It hurt me very much and I had trouble meditating because I could not quiet myself within. I eventually did but my meditation was not as deep. Nevertheless I had lovely Hypnogogic Imagery near the end. I saw two white stars, first one and it grew larger, then disappeared. Then another appeared and did the same. They could have been stars or starfish—but I believe stars. I saw too, a silhouette of a canoe on a lake with trees in background—then two angels one at a time—small then growing bigger then gone! I do not think I ever saw a star in my meditations before and a star has become significant to me in my life for numerous reasons in past months—for almost a year now. I did feel more at peace after meditating but not totally and later I meditated again in late afternoon.

MAY 4, 1995

I wrote a long poem to help myself over what is troubling me. It is less troublesome today after meditating yesterday and today and writing the poem. Prayer, meditation and writing always bring peace and above all my blessed little Rochester here with me now as always.

"IT'S OKAY—I'LL CALL AGAIN"

I do not have a Mother who will phone.
No, I have not known—
That pleasure for sixteen years!

The silence often sears—brings me to tears.
Nor can I dial her as I did before—
She does not live there anymore!
I cannot find her any place—
To hear her voice or see her face.

Jan
May 4, 1995

I cannot include the remaining four stanzas to this poem for they are extremely personal. My Mother went to Heaven September 26, 1978.

Last year on May 4th, I had an unusual "Angel happening." Bob did not hear it—but Chester (my personal Angel) and I were alone in the bedroom and Angel music began out in the hall and came right into our bedroom. Chester sat up from my lap—looked in the direction of the music and then at me. I was not imagining it! It is music I have heard before mysteriously. I wrote a poem about it.

ANGEL NOTES

This morning as I sat in prayer—
A tinkling fell upon the air—
Just in the hall outside my door—
Then in the room there came still more.
Delicate music to my right—
And yet there was no one in sight.

Rochester here upon my lap,
Instantly rose up from his nap—
To listen then along with me—
Faced to his right—and seemed to see.
And when the music stilled—we two—
Stared in each other's eyes; we knew!

For Rochester   Jan
my dear, silent   May 4, 1994
witness to our blessing

MAY 21 1995

Two significant things happened today in my spiritual life. When at Mass I began to have funny feelings inside me. I had felt nauseous when I first woke and once during Mass mid-way through these other feelings began that I find impossible to explain. It seemed like uncomfortable feelings were gently shooting up from my mid-section to different places in my upper body and even up near the back of my throat and right ear. I cannot explain. Maybe it was some sort of indigestion but I never get indigestion. You know me—I thought it was my heart maybe and always think the worse. There was no pain whatsoever—just weird feelings. When the time came for the prayer, "I am not worthy to receive You, but only say the word and I shall be healed," I prayed for all those that I always pray for and so many others I do not even know—and then claimed a healing for myself for what was going on inside me. I ask that He take care of the strange problem. When I received the Body and Blood of Christ I retained them in my mouth till I returned to my seat and thanked Him and swallowed. I knew before I swallowed in my spirit that the feelings I had would be gone once I "received." And that is exactly what happened. From the time I swallowed not a trace of those weird sensations returned. They disappeared! I am writing this in the wee hours of morning and never again from that moment to this did I feel them again. I was healed! It gave me such a wondrous feeling in my soul!

The second thing that occurred is such a miracle too, and is incredible evidence of how my Angels are with me. Because I have always been fond of Indian jewelry since I was a little girl—more recently with my learning more about Native Americans and my reading, I have wanted a turquoise ring to wear on my right hand. It is my birthstone and I felt it connects me to the Native Americans. Who knows I may have such blood in me and I pray I do. I wanted a true stone to wear because I love rocks and stones as Native Americans do. My Mother ring of the birthstones of my six children has become too tight and I have not been wearing it and there has been no opportunity to have it made larger. Because I was going to the PowWow at Tamworth today—last night I asked my Angels if they could find me the perfect ring. There are no other places I go that I can easily find a turquoise ring. I might not have been able to until summer when I seem to go to more stores due to family vacationing here. When I got to the Inn, Fran (Note to readers—Fran is Jessica's mother-in-law,

Michael's mother), after we hugged and greeted each other, showed me
a new ring she had bought for $30.00 at Ames (she had saved to buy
things here) that had been $60.00. It was lovely, but next to it she was
wearing a beautiful turquoise ring that I commented on. It was strange
she showed me her new ring right away (also showing me the turquoise
one because it was next to it) like a sign to me. At the PowWow every
booth I went to I looked for a turquoise ring but the ones I did see were
under glass because they were so big and expensive. I knew I could not
afford them so why ask? After many booths and nearing the end of the
circle of booths and the skies darkening like it was going to rain (it did
soon after) I came to almost the very last booth and in it they had many
rings displayed in open cases. I was so excited! I went in and picked up
one that was round and really more green than turquoise. While holding
it my eyes fell on what was a beautiful ring to me. It was a long oval turquoise stone that would come to my first knuckle and had lined designs
on the sides in the silver—and on the turquoise stone itself it had some
delicate silver filigree designs. I liked it immediately and knew instantly
it was meant for me. I put it on and liked it more. It was a little loose but
I prefer that after my other being tight. (I have worn my Mother ring 33
years or more) When I saw it on I knew it was meant for me. It was the
only one I wanted out of all the rings on the trays and I never picked
another one up. I was so excited and showed it to Bob. He looked at it
and said "Oh, it has a silver unicorn on it." I nearly flipped! I did not have
my glasses on (as usual) and did not know the delicate filigree design was
a unicorn—merely an intricate design, I thought! I was ecstatic! I told
Bob I knew without a doubt the ring was to be mine and the fact there
was a unicorn on it confirmed it. And never in my life have I seen a Unicorn combined with Indian turquoise jewelry. In fact Bob said this same
thing first to me—how unusual it was! But unicorns are associated with
Angels in my spiritual life and many times in my Hypnogogic Imagery and
this was a most fantastic thing. My Angels found the ultimate ring and
showed me it was from them. (I believe Rochester—my Angel— also had
something to do with it in spirit) I even knew in my spirit I would be able
to afford it, that it would not be outrageous in price. It was $15.00—so
reasonable! Imagine! I gave it to her right away. The booth I bought it in
was The Proud American. I liked the ring so much and told the woman
and she was pleased. She said her husband's name was Crow. He was

there. The ring is so absolutely beautiful—and with not only turquoise but a Unicorn! Bob knew my joy and really was so sweet that I was joyful. When I got home we were going to settle down for the evening to read and watch TV and dear Rochester with us—and I told Bob I had to first go upstairs to my prayer/writing room and thank Christ and my Angels for my ring. I am not materialistic and my clothes are so poor, but I am rich in books—my obsession—so this ring was spiritual and unusual for me. I have no expensive jewelry at all. I held my hand out to Christ's sketch on the wall I had made that hangs over my desk and where my little Angel altar is and where my Angel Rochester lies a part of every day as I am writing, and asked that Christ bless my ring and my Angels also bless it. I believe and know that they did and Rochester's precious paw upon it is the dearest and ultimate blessing it could receive. This was such an extraordinary happening to have the ring that was meant only for me, an answer to prayer. It is so symbolic of my spirituality. It means more than I can say. A unicorn is also considered a symbol of Christ. I have read this in a book on the history of unicorns. The turquoise is also significant—my birthstone and linking me to Native Americans and rocks and stones of the earth.

(Postscript: As I transcribe this journal entry now it is thirteen years, one week and six days later, and I am still wearing the Unicorn and turquoise ring. I have worn it continuously every day. Rochester also seems to be a part of it.)

JUNE 8, 1995

I awoke this morning with a line or phrase going around in my mind. This has happened other times and sometimes I do not follow and merely write it down—sometimes I pray about it for interpretation and sometimes like today I decide it is a line for a poem. It seemed instantly to be the first line of a poem so I got my pad and pen right away and the rest of the poem flowed out very easily. The phrase I heard when I woke was: "It seems we live outside of time."

That was unusual and I liked it. I told Bob about it and then showed him the poem and he really liked that too—as well as the one I wrote yesterday for Rochester to celebrate his birthday. (Rochester's poem "Soul's Token" appears in my previous Meditation #4 so I will not include it here again.)

In the following poem there is a line stating how the birds and God's creations teach us and after I wrote it I made mention with an asterisk of the scripture Job 12:7-10 for it states all these things. And the one verse is so wonderful—verse 10. It says: "In His Hand is the soul of every living thing, and the life breath of all mankind." This is one of numerous verses I learned when writing *The Ostrich Syndrome* that speaks of God's Creatures having souls (full title—*Compassion for All Creatures: An Inspirational Guide for Healing the Ostrich Syndrome*).

When I meditated I was startled to see in Hypnogogic Imagery—the very first thing—a large hand with fingers curled gently and the fingers were facing me. Gradually out of the empty hand there arose a large white bird—like an egret or heron. It was exactly like in the verse 10 of Scripture! "In His Hand is the soul of every living thing." I had never seen a hand before in meditation. How incredible—like the scripture verse was being confirmed to me! It was amazing to me! I also saw the large bird again standing in water and I saw a white angel. There was another image I have forgotten due to my excitement over the large hand which I believe to be God's and holding the bird symbolizing "He is holding the souls of every living thing." I cannot stop thinking about how this imagery tied in directly with the line in scripture I associated with my poem. It was like I was being taught and directed from the moment I awoke with being given the first line of the poem that led to the scripture I feel I was supposed to see—followed by the Hypnogogic Imagery. I am grateful and in awe.

Creation's Glories

It seems we live outside of time—
In the woods—and in our prime,
Amongst the birds and with God's creatures—
These and rocks and trees are teachers,*
And the moon that shines on high—
And every glorious, starry sky.

Such gifts create deep gratitude—
We realize the magnitude—

Of wondrous blessings that are ours.
And new today? God's sweet wildflowers!

*Job 12: 7-10   Jan
                                                June 8, 1995

JULY 6, 1995

Since my last entry I learned that Uncle George was ill with cancer (June 27) and then I learned he died July 2nd! I cannot believe it! It has saddened me so much. I have done a lot to extend sympathy and Bob also—and I have talked with his neighbor once and daughter Kathy twice. I have written much to them and we sent flowers—and I sent Kathy a journal with my enclosures. It saddens me so much.

SEPTEMBER 10, 1995

In Hypnogogic Imagery today in meditation I saw an "eye" and lid and lashes twice. At first it was at a slight angle looking to the right (my right and then an "eye" looking straight at me) Then I saw an odd thing—a man on a tractor and he was up close to me with me behind him viewing him so that I only saw the back of his head and back and side of his face. He was bald—no hair at all—and had overalls and Tee shirt on. He said something I cannot remember. I wish I could.

OCTOBER 28, 1995

In Hypnogogic Imagery last night when meditating at the close of it after praying for the Angels to speak to me before meditation, I saw a large Angel in darker gown—maybe a dark red with arms lifted high and she was out over the shoreline of our lake for I saw even the white trellis in foreground. Then her chest seemed to become transparent and a white globe of light could be seen through this transparent area and it floated out over the lake into the heavens and disappeared. That was the end of it.

Later in Hypnogogic Image or an instantaneous mini dream, I saw a sweet little yellow table with turned wooden legs and sitting in the middle of it was a plate of Chester's food. A strange thing—yet it was a pretty picture. Anything to do with Chester is beautiful to me.

Today in meditation I saw two Angels side by side that floated and turned into two horses or two unicorns. It was all so brief I could not tell which—but I had a long meditation time and quite deep in my writing room in early evening.

NOVEMBER 25, 1995

I have been so bad about writing in here and recording things after meditation or that are important in any way in all areas. But I continue to faithfully keep my regular journal but that is so different from this one. And I still have had no time to transfer any of this into my other journal.

One day in Hypnogogic Imagery a week or so ago I clearly saw a woman's face with dark sunglasses and dark hair pulled back and she was hard looking and also chewing gum and it was odd. She appeared several times. I have had more Angel images also in meditation and afterwards.

MUCH LATER

Almost two weeks ago (November 13) I received a surprise letter stapled into a catalog of books from Blue Dolphin Publishing. I had written a query letter there so long ago about my *Ostrich Syndrome (Compassion for All Creatures)*. I was amazed to read this and that they wanted to see chapters of my *Ostrich Syndrome* and also a biographical sketch of myself. I was so overwhelmed. I have it all recorded in detail in my regular journal. Please, dear Christ and my Angels, help me. (Dolphins are thought to be Angelic Beings.) Is it possible my manuscript will be accepted? Is this a sign?

Post Script—Yes, I say with great joy it was accepted and my other thirteen books that I wrote since then were also published by Blue Dolphin and I extend my deepest gratitude to Paul Clemens my publisher and all of his wonderful staff. Bob's and my first book Whispered Notes *was written together before I wrote my other books.*

I end this spiritual note book and journal with a lovely entry—that of a lovely dream that means so much to me and that I will remember forever. I so often cannot remember dreams even though I know and sense when I wake many have been significant—but the Angels must have wanted me to have this dream forever for it was with me the instant I wake. I cherish it! I cannot stop thinking about it all this day.

It was very short. It was unworldly, or should I say "other-worldly" and will nourish my soul from this day forward. It was so realistic even though other-worldly or from another realm.

Rochester comes to be with me daily in our writing room as I work. He naps there on the bed and every so often comes over to me to cuddle, bump heads, sit on my desk to look into my eyes—or to sit on my lap there—or if I am in my soft chair behind my desk and desk chair. With this background I then write this simple precious dream.

Dream: Rochester came to me and began to bump heads and we cuddled and he sat with me awhile and we just enjoyed this closeness.

As he began to get down from my lap I said to him as I always do—"I love you, Chester."

And without hesitation I heard Chester answer—"I know."

In the dream I was stunned and overjoyed for I know Christ and my Angels wanted me to hear Chester say these words to me in English— even though his actions and love and affection speak these words over and over.

Then Chester—in the dream— came back to look at me in the eyes and to knead my shoulders and chest in affection as he has done daily since he was a kitten.

The words he spoke I can hear in my soul clearly and I will have them as my treasure forevermore. Chester spoke these most blessed words to me, I am overwhelmed. He is my soul. We are one soul.

I will not write anymore in this book. I want it to end with that dream. This notebook is filled with so much spiritual treasure—and this was the ultimate—this dream.

Postscript: Later I would write Journal of Love—Spiritual communication With Animals Through Journal Writing as Rochester began to communicate more deeply and teach me to communicate with him. This Journal of Love *followed our* Compassion for All Creatures. *All our books were lovingly typed by Bob after I had written them in long hand*

Postscript #2: Not mentioned in this journal but in my regular journal——is an important fact worthy to enter now.

On my dad's birthday June 2, 1994, I began using Janice Gray Kolb as a new form of my name to honor my dad. I will use my name in this form for all my writing now beginning with Compassion for All Creatures.

THE END

Rochester on the cover of the book
he inspired, as well as the lifestyle
of vegetarianism.

A Journal Entry by Clayton

IT HAS BEEN A SWEET PHENOMENON since summer of 2007 (and it is now summer of 2008) that our three young grandsons have presented us with their personal writings about New Hampshire. Though we have nineteen grandchildren of all ages, these three young boys we always think of as "The October Boys" for they were each born in October, one year apart. Clayton is twelve years old, Cole is eleven and Jameson is ten. These boys are extremely close and bonded and even if they have been apart for long periods there is instant kinship and camaraderie and love the minute one or two are together or the blessing of all three at once. Ball games are started on the lawn here and fishing from dock or kayaks—or just hanging out together talking. These times are special for Clayton lives in New Hampshire, Cole lives in New Jersey and Jameson lives in Rhode Island. Time and distance do not interfere in their abiding friendship. It is always as if they have never been apart.

It is a privilege to me then to include the following writing of a journal entry done by Clayton in his Center Ossipee Grade School here in New Hampshire which is approximately twenty five minutes from our home, and in the town in which he lives. Clayton was born in New Hampshire and for the first seven years of his life lived in the Hitching Post Village Inn in Center Ossipee that I have written of in previous books. He is the son of our daughter Jessica and son (in-law) Michael who were the Innkeepers for ten years. Clayton has two older sisters, Maxine and Renee and a precious dog Isabelle that spends time here often with us I mention in my books and a little cat Critter.

This is a journal-keeping family and Clayton has been writing in one for some time at school and home. When Jessica and Michael ran the Inn Jessica also placed a journal in each bedroom so that guests could write anything they wished in them—and they did. It was all very lovely and the journals are keepsakes. Many guests shared about their lives not only about their enjoyable stay in the Inn.

I cannot end this little introduction without adding there is one other October Boy in this family—the "elder," and he was a lone October boy for many years until the arrival of Clayton. Ryan Alexander Gottlieb is twenty-five and is loved by all, especially the three younger October Boys. He lives in our former hometown of Jenkintown, Pennsylvania and we were just blessed by two visits from him in three weeks with one of his brothers, Jesse. Clayton and Jameson were able to be with him too—but not Cole. Ryan and Cole frequently see each other in Jenkintown.

Ryan Alexander Gottlieb

L to R:
Cole (Nicholas) Wm. VanDorick
and Clayton Walter Drakely

I am so pleased now to present a journal entry of Clayton's just as there will be one by Jameson a little further along in this book. A wonderful poem about New Hampshire written in school by Cole appears in my previous book *Silent Keepers* sent to me before Cole arrived here on vacation last year. All three boys had written about New Hampshire in 2007 though none knew the others did also. Clayton, Cole and Jameson each have two sisters and all the boys love nature and animals and the outdoors. I cannot introduce you to Clayton without telling you that he has ever been a vegetarian and this is Clayton's decision alone.

A JOURNAL ENTRY
WRITTEN BY
CLAYTON WALTER DRAKELY
EARLY FALL 2007
CANOEING

On the last day of summer, my family and I went camping. It was a lot of fun. My favorite part was when my Dad and I went canoeing. We went down the river and I felt ripples in the water like they were waves at the beach. I see bushes flattened by moose and deer like a stampede racing through a meadow of tall grass. I smell the fresh untouched air as if no living being had ever been there. I hear birds calling to each other. The river current rushes against the canoe as if late for an important meeting. I taste the river so peaceful and serene. As we venture down the river I hear a beautiful sound, the sound of a waterfall. It sounds like a shower waiting to be bathed in. I look at Mother Nature and feel the rippling water, see the flattened bushes, smell the fresh air, hear singing birds, taste the river's peacefulness, see the crashing waterfall, and think how lucky I am to be part of it.

—Clayton Walter Drakely

Cousins
Two of the "October Boys"
left to right
Jameson Ronald Kolb,
age 9 years,
and
Clayton Walter Drakely
—author of this Journal Entry
"Canoeing,"
age 11 years,
on "Higher Ground"
by the lake—2007

Journal of Love

Spiritual Communication with Animals Through Journal Writing

—Janice Gray Kolb

XCERPTS AND COMMENTARY on precious experiences recorded in my journal concerning interchanges with Rochester, and plants, birds, trees and all of nature.

Journal of Love

GIFTS OF LOVE

There are some delights in life
Just so precious—
That we are wondrously in awe
That these blessings could actually be,
And that we have been permitted
The caress of a paw—and
To actually see—
And witness, and be recipients of
Holy, reverent, and priceless
Actions—gifts of love—
From our devoted animals
      who are miracles in our lives.

For beloved Rochester
on the date of his estimated
birth in 1986

Jan
April 15, 2008

For things are not mute:
the stillness is full of demands,
awaiting a soul to breathe in
the mystery that all things exhale
in their craving for communion.
　　　　　—Abraham Joshua Herschel in *Music of Silence*
　　　　　by David Heindl-Rast and Sharon Lebell

God speaks to us within our thinking and in all of creation that surrounds us. To speak with nature, the birds, trees, plants, and the animals is not a gift for a select few but is for everyone. We all have this potential if we only are patient and listen. But above all, we must love. And so if we are to communicate with an animal, we must love the animal and the divinity within this creature. Then the communication can begin if we give ourselves to it in love. With the same breath God created us, He created His creatures. Breath, life and soul were known as "Anima" in Latin, and our word "animal" comes from this. We are told in legends about wise and holy people who communicated with animals and have lived peacefully and gently with Animalia, kingdom of the animals.
　　　　　—Jan, *Journal of Love: Spiritual Communication*
　　　　　with Animals Through Journal Writing

This passage you have just read is from the Introduction of a book I wrote and that was published in 2000 by Blue Dolphin. I should say most emphatically it was written by Rochester and me, not myself alone, for he was my inspiration and Angel for all of my books and we communicate. I use the present tense, for the communication did not cease when he went to Heaven. His soul and spiritual presence are in my soul and we have written five books together since he passed on March 8, 2002. This one is our sixth. Also we have written four additional books following *Journal of Love* while he was still here in body as my constant companion and Angel. Actually he and I began writing together in 1986 when he entered my life as a kitten, and two books were written previous to *Journal of Love*. Our oneness is eternal and I carry his Anima within me. It is a gift that is explained in detail in the books written since he entered Heaven beginning with our *In Corridors of Eternal Time*.

I will not explain the wonder of this relationship and the joy and comfort of it all in detail here for it is written about so completely in the books following his passing. I knew we were truly one when he was in body, but to have this gift after his passing is blessing not explainable in human words. I have attempted to say a few lines about it in the present through the poem written recently that opens this segment. I know this gift is eternal. Many more poems are in my previous books.

As I wrote in *Journal of Love*—

What you read in these pages you will either read in disbelief and dismiss as insanity, or you will feel an inner conviction in your heart resonating a soundless yes. Many will know at once it is true. Others will want to believe desperately, for they may have had a slight lifting of "the veil" or "a flash of knowing," but needed a book such as this to bring confirmation to at last accept it joyously. Once accepted it can lead to clear and precious dimensions that seemed only to exist in children's story books.

Since I wrote those words I have read many books by authors who can communicate with animals and I have seen numerous ones as guests on well known television shows. It is authentic, and many animals are helped and comforted through this gift as are humans. That communications from Rochester have continued after he passed have changed my life and beliefs and thinking, strengthening me spiritually that I can never be shaken, enhancing my Christian foundation, and taking away all fears. I have shared my grief and heart and soul in the trilogy I wrote following Rochester's entrance into Heaven, particularly with the first and second books, *In Corridors of Eternal Time* and *Solace of Solitude*. The third, *A Pilgrim on Life's Road*, has much comfort in it also about this journey each of us is making.

But the strongest message that comes from all of this, and specifically from *Journal of Love*, is what I pray you will receive and prayerfully meditate upon. It is this:

If a creature of God could speak to you in words that you could understand as if it were a human speaking, could you then ever eat a creature again?

May we all always practice Ahimsa and attempt to lead others to this highest of spiritual traits. A little marmalade and white cat led me and together Rochester and I have been praying for years that we will be used spiritually to speak to other hearts. And may you then too begin to communicate with animals and let them create the wholeness in your spiritual lives. *The Journal of Love* can gently lead you and you will learn profound truths if you allow your heart to soften and listen.

I am not willing to share Rochester's personal messages to me now in this present book word from word for I feel they should be kept in our original book *Journal of Love*. I know in spirit Rochester agrees. They are meant to be in text with all that the entire book relates in regard to *spiritual communication with animals through journal writing.*

I am willing however to share the essence of a message for it is the true essence of all his messages, that of love.

He tells me that if I do nothing else in regard to sharing our life together it is to relate to humans that they will receive so much love and the unexpected from their animal companions if only they take time to give them quality time as they would to a human friend, and to observe and listen.

He states (in paraphrase here) that animal companions have so much wisdom and love to give if only not ignored, but loved. He tells me that communication should not be the unexpected but the expected.

And I can tell you that this is truth for I have lived it with Rochester for many years before his passing and ever since. I know I shall forever.

I will mention one other message in paraphrase from his *Journal of Love* for he tells me that he knows it gives me great joy when I awake in the night to find him asleep on my tummy or legs. Oh, it does! And he says that it is his way of continually expressing his love and he prefers to sleep there than any other place.

This is profound to me for I could not know then when I received that message and wrote it down and the book was published in 2000 that I would continue to have his presence after he passed upon me on my legs and tummy before, during, and after sleep nightly, and too when I sit on the living room sofa at night my back against the arm and my legs on the sofa to read or watch television. Just as in physical life and presence when Rochester was there upon me every night and evening, so he has continued to be so in spirit since his passing. He began at once to be with me. I have electrical-like vibrational currents and sensations, and great heat when his spirit is present and resting with me. It is a miracle and an enormous gift of eternal love. I have read multitudinous numbers of books on the subject of Afterlife in my grief and need and searching, and I am not alone in experiencing such a gift. It is mentioned by several others but they receive it on occasion and not continuously, and they too feel so blessed. There could be many others. Through Rochester's passing and continual spiritual presence in many other ways as well, I have felt closer connections with my parents and Uncle who are in Heaven, for Rochester has led me to acquire new gifts of awareness, and my life is different. *It is always in the present.* And I experience touches and gifts and visions frequently from beyond. Many have been recorded in my Trilogy and too in my most recent book *Silent Keepers* about my dad and Rochester. It is so important to write things down in a journal and preferably as close to the present moment of the precious gifts that are given and experienced, for though you think you will remember every detail you simply cannot. These are priceless gifts and communications from the hereafter! But moments, days, and years in this life here on earth are also significant and so worthy of being recorded in writing in a journal. I cannot begin to tell you how meaningful and restorative it is to me to write but I am attempting to convey that through this book and many of my previous ones also. Please write!

I have tried in all of my books to write about respect for animals and though the majority of my books are on other subjects, my Rochester is tucked into each. He is my Angel and we began writing books when he entered my life. I have to express whenever I have the opportunity that all God's Creatures should be respected and that includes insects, for no creature is not worthy or too insignificant to be respected. I have seen written poetry for insects, their lives and their passings, as have others. We are all interdependent.

Animals can bestow upon us prayer and healing just as we can for them. I have experienced it deeply through Rochester and written about it in prose and poetry in my journals and books. I have had Rochester lie on me so many times when I have not felt well and he would stay endlessly with me not even leaving me to eat. His little paws often gently held my hands fast and he would purr and look into my eyes to comfort me. These are times that are lovingly ingrained within me.

GUARDIAN ANGEL

Little being filled with love—
You fit my heart just like a glove—
Revealing soul—in silent gaze—
And constant presence through the days.

Waiting in anticipation—
On bathrobed lap—your chosen station,
You remain—to underscore—
You long that I'll be strong once more.

Golden eyes in concentration
Search my eyes in adoration—
Little paws clasp firm my hand,
Telling me you understand.

Purring me to sleep and rest—
To make me well is your sweet quest.
Guardian Angel in soft fur—
White and marmalade comforter.

Dedicated to
Rochester Harry Whittier Kolb (Chester)

Rochester too was always drawn to me when I was praying and
would come to lie close in my lap or to stand on it and put his paws on
the front of me over my heart where love is and bump his little head
onto my forehead to let me know his love and devotion. He would often
knead the area of my heart. He too always held my Rosary when I was
praying it in prayer, often keeping his little paw upon it and my hand as
he laid upon me, so that the Rosary remained stationary. His preciousness often caused tears then and in times since in remembering. I know
he is ever there each time I use my Rosary and it is the Rosary I chose
to always pray during the Holy Hour I spend with him each Friday at 5
PM. It was at 5:07 PM he entered Heaven that terrible Friday, March 8th
and so we pray together especially then and he is ever with me. I have
felt his touches numerous times in this Holy Hour since he passed and

also briefly seen his spirit several times in this Hour. These gifts from him are all recorded in my journals and some in my books. Fridays at 5 PM are Holy, but all times throughout the week that we pray are so Holy and comforting too. Prayer is not limited to Fridays.

And this is our life: find tongues in trees, books in running brooks, sermons in stones, and good in everything.

—Shakespeare

This is a significant quotation that appears in my *Journal of Love* regarding talking with nature which includes all things such as plants, trees, flowers and wildlife. The Australian author Michael J. Roads is one whose book I discovered titled *Talking with Nature* as I was being taught by Rochester to communicate more fully with him.

Like myself, this Australian author keeps journals. He receives his messages through writing! This book is astonishing and I get lost in the wonder of it whenever I reread, and when I first discovered it, it was overwhelmingly confirmative and exciting! It was as if I had been given permission to do what I had occasionally been secretly doing for a long time. I had discovered another soul who wrote wondrous messages in his journals—messages received in mysterious ways. And he believed them! And so I continue to talk to my indoor plants, and if I hear in spirit their name when I ask them then I call them by name. If I do not hear one, I give them a name I feel is appropriate—for I believe the name I choose is inspired in a mysterious way. I also name many trees in like fashion, especially the three enormously tall pine trees that surround the platform that holds my prayer chair by the lake, and significant bushes, and very especially memory plants we have bought for Rochester. His first memorial plant for the first birthday spent without his physical presence with me is a glorious coral Hibiscus that has grown incredibly tall and full. These past two years she now resides permanently indoors by the large front sliding glass door where Rochester used to love to sit and watch the birds and squirrels. She has thrived! Though I have named all his other memory trees and bushes outdoors and some after him (using his middle name and various love names), Bob named this first memory plant before I had prayed about her. (I felt she was feminine) He calls her "Biscus" and he claims I always say "Hi-Biscus" when I greet her for she is a Hibiscus plant. And so "Biscus" she is.

Hibiscus Memorial Plant for Rochester named "Biscus." Wooden statue of Rochester is a gift created by my son-in-law Francis Egan.

Plants and trees do respond to attention in prayer and conversation along with their continuous care. I do pray for and with my plants. One sad and unusual thing has happened in regard to a thriving Christmas cactus here in our living room. Rochester loved to sit by her on the little table and look at the activity out on our deck. She grew and grew and instead of flowering with her bright fuscia flowers only once a year as is normal, she began to flower twice. She loved Rochester's company and our prayers and conversations. Perhaps Rochester prayed for her or with her each time he sat with her. Rochester has a Heart of Love. Then she gradually began to bloom three times and soon four times a year, and her green foliage grew taller and fuller. She added joy and he and I enjoyed her! When Rochester went to Heaven, Winter (that is her name because she came to me at Christmas in Winter) began to fade and drop her blossoms and shrink. It truly was evidence that plants have feelings and not the first time I had experienced this. I have written in my *Journal of Love* of a dear Jade plant simply named Jade dying when I removed her here from her New Hampshire window sill taking her to Pennsylvania in 1993 with me for a short stay at Christmas. I had only one Jade plant back then and decided to take her on the trip. I removed her from her special place and cottage and even to another state so far away. I consider this woods, lake, and cottage my "heart's home," and so I realized too late that this plant also considered it hers. Jade withered in spirit and body when I took her from New Hampshire and her window that looked out over the lake and woods. I was crushed when I brought her limp and dead back to our home. I had taken care of her in Pennsylvania in all the same ways I took care of her here. She could not bear to be removed from our cottage. This spoke to my soul and made me more attentive to my plants. They are really not much different than we are. She passed away in her desire for her New Hampshire home before I could bring her back here to her favorite window. I too, would wither in spirit whenever I would have to leave our home in the woods. I wrote a poem for her and I was so sad. I felt I had killed her! I had! It was terrible. I share this poem again that appeared in *Journal of Love*.

ODE TO JADE—OF NEW HAMPSHIRE

I had a little rubber plant
   She sat upon my sill
I prayed for her and talked to her
   But then against her will—

I took her to another state
   So we'd not be apart.
She thought this was her cruel fate—
   The move just broke her heart!

I watched her droop and then she sighed—
   I did not mean to kill!
Oh yes, her little spirit cried—
   Upon that foreign sill!

I prayed for her and talked to her—
   I told her we'd return—

She sat so limp and did not stir
　Oh, how her heart did yearn!

Through selfishness I surely slayed—
　Her home had been denied!
That little rubber plant named Jade,
　Just shriveled up and died.

When we are given a Heart's Home—
　And this I know is true!
Let no one ever make you roam—
　Your spirit can die too.

Dedicated to Jade　　　　　　　　　　　　Jan
　　　　　　　　　　　　　　　　　　March 9, 1994

　　Winter, the Christmas Cactus did not die as Jade did but she became smaller and shorter and less full and never ever bloomed again since 2002. She grieves for Rochester though I feel he visits her in spirit on the piano back in front of the sliding glass window. And I talk and pray with her each day. I even placed a small framed picture of Rochester next to her just as he once sat next to her in body. I know he visits with her in spirit but Winter just cannot rise up and be as before. Grief remains. I understand. Biscus sits on the low table now that Winter and Roches-ter once shared due to Biscus's huge size. I think she grows in actuality and spirit because she is Rochester's. There are many other true stories I could tell you about plants and trees and birds and animals but they can be read in *Journal of Love* and my other books written since then even when the book's subject matter is not about them. When you live in nature in a woods by a lake, Mallards and Squirrels and Plants and Trees often wander into the pages unannounced and I can never turn them away. They bless my spirit and are spiritually delightful. and they lived here before I did. I believe the animals and the plants and trees and all creatures of earth pray and recognize that God is their source. That is my strong feeling and that far more than we can yet understand is taking place right before our eyes when we are in an animal's presence (especially our personal companions) or in a garden or woods. I have had experiences here that are so beautiful and otherworldly. Each night at dusk I say good night to all the flowers in the seven gardens and talk to them and the trees as I walk around. Bob, who often overhears from the porch, will say, "Who were you talking to?" and smile. He knows. I ask all here in our woods to pray for themselves and each other and for us. I believe too as I plant gardens here they too are being planted in Heaven and are far more beautiful, and Rochester and I will walk in them together as he does now with my dad, who cares for him while I am still on earth.

Others talked to nature too—great men who were recognized and believed and honored. George Washington Carver was a man I have admired ever since reading about him as a child. He was born just before the Civil War and was a genius and an agricultural chemist. He accepted as natural and normal that plants were able to reveal their hidden secrets upon request. I have written about him at length in my *Journal of Love* and he is delightful to know. I am in awe when I read about him. He stared at a peanut plant and asked, "Why did the Lord make you?" And in an instant he received the briefest of answers and shared all he learned with agricultural specialists. Carver believed everyone can do the things he did if only they believe it. He believed all the secrets were in the Bible in God's promises. He believed when he touched a flower he was touching infinity and through that flower he talked to the Infinite. I too believe they are of God. He believed in the invisible world and in fairies as do I. Carver had his own Masters Degree and was brilliant and solved many agricultural problems in the South. He had his own private little laboratory which he christened "God's Little Workshop" and he would sit in there communing with plants for hours. He took very early morning walks before sunrise to commune with nature and the plants that spoke to him and he said God talked to him and told him plans to fulfill. These are only snippets of his life story. More are in *Journal of Love* and other books about his life written by others.

Luther Burbank is another amazing man I wrote about in *Journal* and he is worthy of being investigated. He would get down on his knees and talk to plants when he wanted them to develop in some particular way not common to their kind. And they did! His life and work and communication with plants is quite incredible and I am not going to include it here other than to direct your interest to him and you can read more fully about him in my *Journal* or other books. He had exuberance of a small boy and wonder for all things about him. He said his body was no older than his mind—and his mind was adolescent. He said it never grew up and he hoped it never would. This too describes myself—one who remains interiorly like a child in many ways and who is filled with the wonders of animals and nature. Each of us too can be like a "wise child" that can understand the language of flowers and trees and animals. Burbank explained to a friend that he took plants into his confidence, and he asked them to help, and he affirmed them and assured them he held their small lives in deepest regard and affection. There are many others too in the past who believed in the Divinity of each living thing and too in the present. I am not alone in this belief.

You may wish to read about the Findhorn Garden also, a small spiritual community in the north of Scotland. At Findhorn they talk to the plants in the garden, and the plants seem to like it so much they respond by growing out of sand and blossoming in the snow. You may wish to read more about this miraculous garden in various books that have been written about it or in my *Journal*. The book I own about it is titled *The Findhorn Garden by the Findhorn Community* (Harper and Row Publishers, 1975 First Edition) These messages received from the plants and vegetables and Deva and Angels and Nature Spirits only make me realize all the more how important it is to attempt communication with our animal friends and to pray with them and realize that they are of God and love Him. We feel that Love.

These messages are in the same lovely worded intelligent form as Rochester's messages are to me and as Michael J. Roads received from all his contacts with various forms of nature and animals. He wrote the messages in his journal as did I, and George Washington Carver, and Luther Burbank, and yes, even Henry David Thoreau. He impressed and affected me in his book *Walden* and I mention Thoreau's particular influence on me in a book I wrote previous to *Journal of Love* entitled *Higher Ground*. Luther Burbank was also lastingly impressed by Thoreau.

In my mentioning Michael Roads and his contacts with nature spirits and deva, and George Washington Carver who believed in fairies, it seems appropriate to tell you that Rochester and I had a song—*our song*. Years ago Chester and I were given the ethereal music of *The Fairy Ring* by Mike Rowland that we entered together before sleep each night, music I have written about in previous books. This music I played continually for thirteen years after it was given to me in 1989 by a dear friend Ruth. It is not music to read by or write by or use as background. It is for us, music for the night and aloneness, and shared only with Rochester and Bob. It did not appeal to Bob after many playings (and even originally, but he thought it would eventually end and I would stop playing it). Thirteen years later it was still playing each night, but in all fairness he goes to sleep so quickly he does not realize it is on. I know only that the haunting strains were so healing to me through the years and to Rochester also. He never liked loud music or when Bob played the piano, for Bob plays so well, but with great force, volume and gusto—especially our hymns. Rochester would immediately leave the room. I have written about *The Fairy Ring* in detail in other books but felt it significant to enter here. It especially calmed and soothed Chester after our 430 mile trips we would make so frequently back and forth to New Hampshire in the years before 1996 when we finally moved here in January. I long to hear that music now for it may bring unexpected solace as it has done in other situations, but I have been afraid to play it since Rochester's passing even though he is ever with me. He would put his little white paws into my hands as he and I drifted off to sleep. He still does and always shall. Bob has made so many extra copies of this tape through the years for we kept wearing it out and I could never find another in a store. The cassette sits in the player since 2002 waiting to be heard. Perhaps soon. *The Fairy Ring* is our music, our song. It is a blessing to us. (I write in the present tense. Rochester is ever present.) And Rochester is pure blessing to me above any music.

Birds should be appreciated and listened to also for they can be easily heard and detected communicating. The crows in particular are so interesting to me and they appeared to me in very mystical ways after the passing of Rochester. I have written of it in previous books. In their conversations with each other too, and in their calling out, they "caw" in a series. In the woods we hear them regularly and one crow might "caw" four times in a row and almost immediately an answer will come in a series of four from another part of the woods. This goes on and on in various numbers for I have been paying attention through the years and counting the caws of interchanges.

Crows are said to be extremely intelligent birds. They have made very deliberate and spiritual and haunting appearances to me on our front deck since Rochester went to Heaven and also keep vigils on specific days that are significant to me in regard to Rochester. It has been a mysterious and comforting awakening for me in regard to crows, and other birds too. My special friend Connie, knowing their significance in my life and my extraordinary love for Rochester sent me a handsome nearly life-size black Crow carved in wood with a golden star dangling from his beak. It is not possible to explain how much this carving means to me, for it is a symbol of the faithful crows who have been in solemn attendance on the deck since Rochester passed, and the Star is my Rochester. A picture of this crow appears in my book *Pilgrim*. It truly is a message of love and hope, an additional sign that another realm is just beyond the veil. There is so much we can come to know if we take the time to listen and observe and talk to birds and animals either silently or aloud. I have carried on conversations and made spiritual connections through the glass sliding doors with the Mallards and Blue Jays and others. Rochester and I would often sit together and watch them through the sliding glass doors in winter and through the screens in summer, and they were delightful. So much can be learned from them. I continue to watch them with Rochester in spirit. They have appeared to me in incredibly surrealistic ways since his passing and I feel God through the birds. The Crows especially in these woods have held messages for me in spirit for I will ever remember the two Crows who kept vigil for Rochester for over a year on our deck. They still come but not as intensely. Numerous times a week. I have written of their deeper message in *Corridors*. Author Brad Steiger has stated that a Crow "is one that watches shrewdly over the lay of the land on both spiritual and physical levels" (from *The Transformative Power of Your Personal Animal Totem*).

I write of spirit photography in my book *Pilgrim* which I will only touch on here, just enough to encourage you to look carefully at your own pictures. I have told of this in detail but I will just say briefly I took two pictures of one of the Crows that kept vigil and when they were developed, one photo was normal except for the faint white area above the crow. The second picture made me stare in wonder for there above the black crow on the deck were two clearly defined images in white of two other crows, one on the left at the top and one on the right. They were facing each other and the living crow was beneath (picture is in *Pilgrim*).

I had read of spirit photography and experienced taking some several years ago, but because this picture pertains to Rochester and his Crows who keep watch it overwhelmed and made me cry. It is so significant to me. There is more to read on this subject in *Pilgrim* but be certain to look carefully at your own photos after they are developed, for what may seem to be an imperfect picture can really be a flash of spirit image and light and a greeting from the spirit world. Again, this is a form of communication through birds and nature pointing you to God who is everlastingly there watching over you and encouraging you to be aware and to realize how we are all part of His vast world, both here and hereafter. Such blessings.

In the marvelous book *Kinship with All Life*, the author J. Allen Boone, has established an incredible relationship with a German Shepherd dog named "Strongheart." This is a story and revelation unto itself in addition to all other that is in the book. But in attempt to summarize his experiences here which you can read on your own if you wish, he comes to the conclusion that he and Strongheart were living instruments and for these thoughts to flow between human and dog, the human involved had to have understanding of "the Divinity within all life which innately relates each of us to every living thing and every other living thing to us—in true kinship" (*Kinship with All Life*, J. Allen Boone).

There is another book I have mentioned in many of my recent books and the author Martin Scott Kosins has written precious words for the back covers of three of my own books and is a special spiritual friend. His *Maya's First Rose: Diary of a Very Special Love* (you see, again a Diary [Journal] to express deep love and thoughts) is a uniquely precious book of inspiration for anyone who has ever loved and lost an animal companion.

Martin sacrificed career and friends only wishing to be with Maya. His most important goal was to keep Maya joyful and alive in her final years. He loved her for eighteen wondrous years before she died of old age. He will love her for all eternity. But as did J. Allen Boone and his companion, Strongheart, who sat shoulder to shoulder in shared contemplation under the stars in wonder, Martin and Maya too would sit shoulder to shoulder gazing straight ahead watching all of nature and listening to the call of the geese. They sat beneath a small tree that stood beneath ancient pines and shared love that cannot be put into words. Martin writes, "There was no us anymore. We had become one. Our hearts had a single beat. And our lives a single purpose—the care and companionship of each other." This deep communication existed and shall live in their hearts forever. His thoughts capture my deepest thoughts about Rochester and I had first read these thoughts in his book long before Rochester passed. I have read this book through tears again and again until I have lost count, and too, have given many copies as gifts to friends and I always shall.

My Star

I gaze up at the heavens
    and see the brilliant, shimmering stars
        in the night sky—
And in wonder feel that I
    am one
        with all creation.
And yet this inward elation
    cannot compare
        to what I feel
When I gaze upon the radiant star
    who shares my nights and days—
        shining his love in tender ways
           everywhere we are!
He is my Angel of Light
    my one true star—
        more beauteous
           than all the stars of night.

For Rochester   Jan
with inexpressible love   May 19, 1998
on his birthday
May 30, 1998

Rochester and I shared deepest love and prayer in many forms and he truly was aware of the Divine in our daily life, our little prayers and rituals, in the spiritual objects that surround us (for they still do)—the pictures and statue of Jesus, the statues of the Blessed Mother Mary, St.

Martin DePorres and St. Francis of Assisi (both Saints who loved animals so and animals are with them in these statuary forms), and Angels. I know that while on earth Rochester was deeply spiritual and was drawn to devotional objects that were around him ever since he was a kitten and he visibly shared his interest in them with me, and that he would come to me when I was inwardly praying or when using a Rosary. He loved to lie on my desk near spiritual objects that were there; statues, pictures, a wooden beaded Rosary. He is pictured sitting on my desk in front of the window with the lake beyond on the cover of *Journal of Love*.

Before moving to New Hampshire permanently In January 1996, I had a prayer and writing room also in that home in the former room belonging to our son. It surely did not have a beautiful view of lake as my present one has, but Rochester liked to sit at one of the windows there too, but not because of the view. There was a table in front of the window I considered an altar with a statue of the head of Jesus and a small wooden icon of Mary and other smaller devotional items. Chester would always sit beside the head of Christ and seemed to be meditating while staring at me. He would sit unmovable there for long periods. I knew he felt a certain peace there before he would eventually leave the statue and come lie on my lap. There was agony on the face of Christ and I had been drawn to it and purchased it while I was in a period of deep emotional pain. I knew Rochester understood.

Rochester at window with statue of Jesus (and icon of Mary and Jesus only partially seen)—a place he liked to sit as a very young cat in my prayer room in Pennsylvania.

We also communicated in love with the blinking of our eyes all through our physical life together. I wrote a poem about this preciousness that appears in my *Compassion for All Creatures*, which has a handsome close-up picture of him on the cover. I will include the poem here. It tells all that I am trying to say now.

SENDING KISSES

Across the room his eyes meet mine
And capture them in fond embrace.
And I blink twice in sweet response
Twice kiss his furry little face.

For eyelids slowly closed and raised
Are kisses to a little cat—
He sends them back with golden eyes—
And bonds me to him just like that!

For those who dwell within this realm—
Of creature love and friendship dear—
Know it is a gift from God
That keeps His Presence ever near.

As I would blink my eyes slowly to Chester I would think the phrase "I love you" ("I" before the blink, "love" during, and "you" after the blink). I learned of this when he was a kitten and read it in Anitra Frasier's book, *The Natural Cat*. From the first moment I read it and put it into practice, Rochester and I confirmed all she had written about "sending kisses" and we spent our life together doing it. It is a very tender encounter. It was on a particular tryst one October evening when we did this that I wrote the poem when he was very young. He then no longer was able to bear the distance and joined me to curl up on my lap. This always happened. He would come to me. The responses from some other cats when I lived in Jenkintown, Pennsylvania and not in the woods, were varied and sweet. I tried to break the language barrier about town with several other cats and succeeded (though not in the same deep way I sent kisses to Rochester). One little cat after such an exchange through my open window looked surprised as he sat on the pavement staring at me in my car. As

I got out of the car to visit a friend, the little cat then rolled over on his back to me in complete trust, a most unusual surrender to a stranger and I stooped in trust also, to pat him.

If you truly love your animal companions, there are so many special means of growing into a very deep relationship. The animal is the greatest teacher, and if we spend time with them we are taught by them in a quite natural way. They truly do have methods of communicating with us, if we only give them our undivided attention and time. They are so worthy. I was taught by Rochester. He was never an inconvenience. I wrote books while he laid upon the very sheets of paper I was writing on. I would gently pull out each finished sheet from under his body. I could never ask him to leave. I would hug him and kiss his little face. His purring was my background music. He often held my pencil still as he did my Rosary as if to help me. I would now give all I can imagine simply to have him here in body again doing those sweet things and desiring my company. He chose to be with me. And he taught me and prayed with me. And he still chooses to be with me and teaches me and prays with me.

There seems to be a delicate divine thread that the Angels use to weave and link so many things in nature and the creature world and mine together, creating spiritual and mystical magic often unexplainable. And Rochester is in the midst of it all.

> *To feel and speak the astonishing beauty of things—earth, stone and water, beast, man and woman, sun, moon and stars.*
>
> —Robinson Jeffers

I did not speak of rocks and stones in this segment of my journal for I might have gone into too much detail. They mean much to me and are discussed in *Journal of Love* and other of my books like *Beneath the Stars and Trees* in detail.

But as with flowers and birds and all forms of life, these are containers of spirit and the divine. Most humans see them as lifeless forms, but they are extraordinary carriers of the divine. They too hold beautiful mysteries carried down through the ages. It is true.

Who can imagine or express what my little Rochester felt or perhaps even saw as he sat next to the statue of the head of my deeply pained Christ in Jenkintown, or held still my Rosary with his paw. I would reflect upon this again and again as I looked into his precious face. He was very young then. Once we moved to New Hampshire the statue was never again seen. It had somehow been lost in transition. I never spoke of it again to Rochester. We were advancing on into a deeper journey and new ways of communication. Beyond even the always ethical treatment and special physical care I gave him, and psychologically in peace of mind and heart, that to provide the spiritual care of this tender soul Rochester whom, I deeply love beyond words, was of the utmost importance. It is meant for all animals. Now he too (as he did then in body) provides deep spiritual care to our one soul.

I could write and write endlessly on the subjects I have written about in my *Journal of Love*. But since the passing of Rochester and because of him I have been taught so very much more in regards to this life and Afterlife and this journey. I am totally different. I live in the moment and am taught. I experience teachings and touches from Rochester and inspiration from Jesus and Mary continuously and am so blessed. I too have a new closeness with my parents and uncle in Heaven.

Love is the most important thing. Love! Everything in life is interconnected from the tiniest bugs and leaves and earth and flowers to the precious animal companions in our homes to those creatures elsewhere—and most humans pay all of this wonder so little regard. I have witnessed again and again on our property humans walk past a group of Mallards so large they cannot be counted (close to one hundred), and it is as if they are invisible. Or a precious squirrel, bird or chipmunk go entirely unnnoticed. Some are even spoken of as annoyances! There is no reverence for these precious gifts from God who are all a part of Him. And I read and read and write and write, and journals and books continue to be written, and I observe and listen as I write. There is so much within you, and all around you and too, unseen. Give time and notice to your own animal companion's spirituality especially and things related—for they have, I believe, an innate love for the Divine. They just love you so much, and time and again they subtly and sometimes overwhelmingly show you their love and devotion and care and so deeply appreciate yours for them. You will experience amazing exchanges when you stay in the present moment and are fully aware, and love!

Please open your eyes and heart—and always write! You will understand once you begin and if you already write, you know. All the people mentioned in this meditation were people who knew the importance of writing down their thoughts and experiences in journals and books so they are ever recorded for their own treasure and benefit, and so they may help others to realize there is so much more, more than we can see with our eyes. We must also see and experience and believe and act upon what we are shown in our hearts by God.

WITHIN

Your love grounds
surrounds
confounds.
You live within
in silence
where the din
cannot reach.
It is there
you teach
and love abounds.

I whisper your name
my heart is its frame
and each letter
is embroidered
forever tightly.
I hear it within
where in a flame
of love
it burns
so brightly.

For
dear Rochester

Jan
October 31, 2003

Rochester in company of Gabriella the Angel
shortly after the statue was given to us.

The Angel was dangling her tiny feet into the round shell font intended to hold water for the birds.

The Cherub Angel was named Gabriella, and Maraglo is the name of the bird from a poem by E. B. White that she is holding.

We kept Gabriella indoors in our living room throughout winter after receiving her as a gift from our Clancys, but in the last week of May we placed the statuary in a garden by the beach.

Rochester sat often daily with Gabriella in the winter months she was indoors. It was very sweet to see.

Isabelle (our
"granddogger")
loved to lie near
the statue of
St. Francis.

MEDITATION SIX

Necessities and Accessories

*Walt Whitman has written a line in his poetry "we are multitudes" and
in writing in our journals we discover who the multitudes are within us.
It takes years but it is worth the writing and prayer.*
—Jan, *Beside the Still Waters*

ALWAYS CHOOSE A PEN that is compatible to the paper pages used
within your journal be it a fountain pen, or rolling writer or ball
point. This too applies to the color ink you prefer. I write in only green
ink as I may have stated elsewhere. Since 1989 all my journals have
been written with Pentel's Rolling Writer (medium point) and Uniball
by Sanford (fine point) and in all other writing I do use these also except
for my pencil written manuscripts. The Pentel I use the most. The Pentel
is a green cased pen and Uniball is black cased. All contain green ink
for that is nature's color and I live in the green woods. They are smooth
writing pens and writing in green speaks to me of animals too and our
vegetarianism we began in 1989 also. The only exception three times
each year is to use violet ink on my mother Violet's birthday, wedding
anniversary and anniversary of "death."

Some people now keep journals on a computer, and if this is better
for you that is fine. But I am speaking of actual writing by hand in a
journal, which gives a certain release and a good feeling that can only
be experienced by doing it. Also you can keep your journal with you to
use anytime you wish and this is important for it should be your confi-
dential friend.

Often the more we journal we are moved beyond words and it is
then we may want to try to draw the images that we see internally. It is

often surprising to learn we can make such drawings if we were never inclined to do so before. These drawings are a form of journaling and will become precious to you. You may wish to use the different drawing materials, pens, pencils, brushes, paint etc. that you keep in your sacred space. You will treasure what you are led to draw on your lined or plain sheets in your journal or in separate art tablets.

I once saw several books in my favorite bookstore in Sanford, Maine before it had to close forever (Bookland) and they were large journals and each a collection of drawings done on lined paper resembling legal pads. In the publishing of them they were housed in hard covers. The interesting thing about them was each drawing done by a person out west or a Native American long, long ago was done on this lined paper but drawn horizontally over the printed lines. The lines then became vertical in their drawings by the turning of the lined pad. They were incredibly beautiful and in great detail and the way these men journaled in those early days—through their art and line drawings. Amazing!

Some years ago I wrote a poem concerning drawing. I have learned to see the simplest wildflower or weed or leaf as exquisitely beautiful and as a potential drawing. Often one becomes an actual sketch in my sketch book or on a page in my journal. Sketching and drawing have remained a part of my life to give simple enjoyment, all because of my solitary and artful imaginations of childhood. To me it has always been part of writing. I began by drawing when I could not yet write as I have shared in my book *The Enchantment of Writing,* and then just incorporated it into life. The art became less essential and the writing became overwhelmingly necessary. But they have the same root in my life, one just flowered into a larger and more fragrant bloom. I could not live without writing. Therein lies the significant difference.

ANOTHER PRAYER FORM

I had not sketched for some time—now
More recently—somehow—
I have been drawn to pencil and pen
And blank paged journal once again—
To record what I am seeing—
To increase my sense of being.

My precious companion—faithful friend—
Now stretches leisurely end to end
Across the pages of my sketch book—
While most admittedly—I look
Upon that dear cat I adore
To simply capture—and underscore
More of his sweetness that I know—
To reveal the truest cameo.

Wildflowers also have their chance
As I stand and sketch and glance
Toward these lovelies—exquisite and meek—
To draw gentle beauty at its peak.
And rippling lake and rocks and grasses—
And the pine cone that surpasses—
In causing interest—all most unique—
Present as gifts their own mystique.

Yes, all that surrounds me is confirmation—
That to write and draw—is meditation.

Dedicated to   Jan
Writing and Drawing
and to pens, pencils
and paper

Writing or drawing in journals has a long history. May you become
part of this and write in your journal what it means to you.

St. Francis statue
in my garden and
flowers growing wild,
done in late 1990s

Colorful Garden

A JOURNAL WHOSE COVER is a beautiful colorful garden and a stone walk way through it with several tall trees in the background. It is bordered by green ferns and the entire hardback back cover is of green ferns. It is tiled Woodland Garden. I too have woodland gardens.

BEGUN JULY 21, 1999
COMPLETED FEBRUARY 9, 2001

This journal has many extremely personal entries so I had to edit it. It was a difficult time, in part, in my life.

Inscriptions in inside cover:

The journal is a writing meditation, a walking meditation,
a mystical journey.
—Burghild Nina Holzer, *A Walk Between Heaven and Earth*

It is important
to honor our beginnings
to remember that we matter,
and that we have
a place in this world
that no one else has"
—Inspired by the Native American Indians

A picture of the cover of my book *Compassion for All Creatures* with my precious Rochester on the cover is glued on the next inner page opposite the first page to make an entry.

Beneath it is a picture of an Angel holding a heart wreath and in a purple gown.

The verse of scripture reads: "Do not forget to entertain strangers, for by doing so some have entertained angels without knowing it." Hebrews 13:2

HIGHER GROUND
WEDNESDAY, JULY 21, 1999

I have just completed a journal earlier today and did not want any time to lapse before beginning a new one. I had many I had bought on hand to choose from but this one I had prepared with pictures inside some months ago so I decided to use this. Also the cover is lovely and appropriate for this time of year and the garden is symbolic of the gardens I create—and will still be creating more.

The news just came through on television that is carrying round the clock coverage, that all three bodies have been found in the water of John F. Kennedy Jr., his wife Caroline and her sister Lauren. At first only he was found earlier this morning with part of the fuselage of the plane. That they could find all three in the vast ocean is incredible. It is so tragic. Thank you Jesus, the families will now see their loved ones and have a Mass for them and a burial. Oh, it is so sad. I cannot begin to record how this is affecting everyone around the world and myself.

I have to get back to work now on an article I was asked to write by author Brad Steiger. I must finish it and mail it next week, just as I will my own new manuscript.

LATER

I called Rob Nelson (from Bookland) and had a very nice conversation with him. I will write about it later. I will miss him at Bookland. He is a great guy and I am so appreciative for all he did for me, plus I feel fortunate to know him.

Ted Kennedy and other family members went by boat to the site of where the bodies of John, Caroline and Lauren were brought up. There is a tremendous reaction all over the world. People are so affected by these deaths of three young people. Thank you Jesus that they stayed together in this tragedy—that their bodies were not lost and separated from each other. In the vast ocean it is so incredible they could find them and in such a short time. Thank you, Jesus.

Later

Their bodies will be cremated and scattered at sea. This amazed me considering they were lost and died in the sea and now once brought out they are going to be returned to the sea. I am sure I will understand once it is explained. The coroner said that all three died of multiple trauma—that is the diagnosis. It is so terrible. Lines and lines of people have waited to put flowers and notes outside their apartment building in New York. They wait in silence. The scene is overwhelming. I am sorry my writing is off the lines slightly two pages previous but I was upset and also writing in the semi-dark without a light.

Today earlier an unusual thing happened. A chipmunk got onto the screened in porch, probably through a hole in the screen that I repaired several times, but the tape does not hold well and up until this incident Bob did not fix it in a better way. Chester chased the chipmunk into the house and under the piano! It all happened so fast (Bob was near the door at the time) we were not even sure it was a chipmunk but maybe a mouse. When Bob moved the piano after I first locked up Chester in the bedroom with the door closed, the little creature ran to outside our closed bedroom door. Bob found him behind a wash basket there and the little chipmunk ran through the kitchen and out on the porch. Bob left the screen door open and the chipmunk ran outside—or we assumed so because we could find him nowhere on the porch. We waited awhile to be sure before I let Chester out on the porch again. We made a fuss over him as we always do when he chases a mouse too. I thank him for protecting us. Of course we would never hurt any little creature nor does Chester. Ever! It was an adventure!

Thursday, July 22, 1999

Birth of Janna's and Bill's baby!

Joy of joys—Janna had her baby early this morning. We got the call around 3 AM. I am so happy to announce the birth of:

Rebecca Mae VanDorick
5 lbs 5 ozs
19.5 inches long.

What a beautiful name! They chose Janna's and Jessica's middle names! Such a beautiful name! She is a tiny weight like Janna was and has dark curly hair and I think, blue eyes. Janna did well though it was very difficult, and did not need a C section as with Dahlia. Janna is so happy as are we and Billy talked to us too. We are so thankful it is over and that Janna is safe and the baby is perfect. Welcome dear little Rebecca Mae!

In direct contrast to this precious birth—John F. Kennedy, Jr., his wife Caroline, and sister-in-law Lauren were all laid to rest in the sea today in a very special ceremony on a ship. Only immediate family were there yet it was televised all day—the preceding events and long after. Apparently it had been John's wish to be cremated had he died and put in the sea. That he died there too is so, so sad. After they retrieved the three bodies autopsies were done last night and the families were able to be with them, and then they were cremated. It is so sad I cannot stand it. We kept the TV on very low all day even though we were doing other things—just to be in spirit with them—in contrast to our never putting the TV on during the day normally. These deaths have deeply saddened me.

FRIDAY, JULY 23, 1999

Today Julia, Maxine, Renee and Clayton were down here all day and I made them lunch and dinner and then Bob took them home at 7:30 PM. They had so much fun swimming and playing and Julia also brought her knitting as did Maxine. The knitting is all straightened out now. They had made mistakes along the way and I helped them the other day. I had to take Maxine's all off the needles and then she began again. She only made two mistakes today and Julia's pink scarf is growing longer. We had a great time together and it was Claytons first time down here with us without Jessica and he did so great. He is a cheerful and loving little boy—a joy!

Bob picked them up in the morning and also took them home. There was not room for me in our red Mitsubishi. We had a nice evening and just relaxed and read and watched TV.

SATURDAY JULY 24, 1999
DENNIS' BIRTHDAY

Have been going over my manuscript again and now at last I believe Bob is going to read it. I have waited all these months for him to read it. It has to be mailed Wednesday (July 28) the day I met Christ in 1991. I cannot believe I have written this entire book. There is so much in it!

Bob and I went to the Post Office, then had breakfast on the porch. It is raining today but a nice rain—sometimes extremely heavy rain, other times showers and occasional sun. It is a "rainforest day" as I call such a day.

I called Barb to say we wanted to take her and Frank out to dinner one night they are here and just to see how she is, but got their message machine and left the message. At the same time I called Laurel and we had fun. I told her we wanted to buy a cot for Jesse to sleep on. She had asked if she could borrow one of our trundle beds but they do not fold. This will be better for her to get a new bed for Jesse. Richard was there too and Laur and I had fun on the phone. I am sorry I made a mark on this cute little dog's head. Even though it is only green ink it bothers me. (There is a sweet dog's picture glued at the bottom of the page.)

Today is Dennis' 48th birthday and we are sorry the Clancys are not up here this weekend. We called Patti and Dennis to tell them about the birth of Rebecca Mae (on Thursday). They were sweet about it.

SUNDAY, JULY 25, 1999
BARBARA'S BIRTHDAY

It is hard to believe Barbie is 40. I remember the day and events of her birth so clearly. Why do the years pass so quickly? I love them all so much. We eventually got her and had a nice talk.

MONDAY, JULY 26, 1999
STEPHEN'S BIRTHDAY

Another milestone I cannot believe! Stephen is 21! Our first grandchild! I felt so young when he was born (I was) and Janna had only just turned nine years two months before. I was still a Mom raising my children—and suddenly a Grandmom too! Stephen is coming up here soon. Wonderful! We talked to him today.

The 7th anniversary of meeting Christ at Immaculate.

Today on this Anniversary—a day in 1992 I will never forget. I sent in my manuscript that I completed entitled *The Enchantment of Writing: Spiritual Healing and Delight Through the Written Word.* I am in awe that I wrote it and it has so much in it to help people. I completed it in very early June but made a lot of additions. It also became a very traumatic time in mid-June. I put my manuscript aside for weeks not able to read it or work on it. I finally made all the additions and did the rereading. Though Bob typed it he never read it as I hoped except for the chapter "Irregular People." It is obvious why he read that. I am sending it all in without him reading it. He says he will begin reading it in the next several days. I am so appreciative for all his typing. I cannot say how appreciative! I truly am! But it does hurt me he will not read my hand-written manuscript when I first complete them. He always tells me how beautiful my handwriting is and tells others too, yet he does not want to read my manuscripts until he types them. Therefore it is not reading the manuscript fresh—like it is when I newly complete it. He sees lots of things I have written as he types yet he says he does not absorb them and often types the chapters out of order. But I have to wait months before he will read my newly written book and this hurts me. And I sound like a big baby and should just shut up! We are just so different. I love writing in long hand and have loved writing since I was a child and can write hours and hours and my hand never tires. And Bob compliments me on this often for he does not enjoy writing. Even if I learned to type, it is his computer (yes ours—but I do not use it. But my manuscripts are typed on it by Bob and that is significant)—and I would keep him from using it for many reasons. He *wants* to type the manuscripts! He waited long to read my books *Higher Ground* and *Compassion* and *Journal of Love* also. I feel like I am a bad person even writing about it for I am so appreciative of all he does! I feel though I honor him by asking him to read, for I do not ever ask anyone else. I trust and value his opinions even though we are extremely different. But I have confidence in this work I have done and written even without Bob reading it. He will read it after I send it! I am proud of it and I know it will help people. It has meant so much to me to write it. I have "laid hands" on the manuscript again before sending it and I thank Jesus in advance every day and night in prayer that it is accepted for publication. I think perhaps Jesus is trying to tell me that I must have more confidence in myself. But I am so appreciative for every page Bob has typed for me and I thank him frequently. He knows I am appreciative!! I thank him so often and never take it for granted. We agreed to work in this way from the very beginning; I write—he types.

I am so grateful for the day I met Christ at Immaculate in Jenkintown and it changed my life. I have written about Him and our meeting in my book *Journal of Love: Spiritual Communication with Animals Through Journal Writing.* Thank you, dear Christ, for all that you do for me and thank you for taking care of Rochester and for watching over this manuscript and for its acceptance. I do not know why I was chosen to meet you that morning seven years ago but I have been ever grateful that I did. I love you, dear Christ. Thank you for loving and protecting Rochester. Thank you for loving and protecting Bob. And myself. Thank you for inspiring me to write this book and for being with me and through the writing of it. I am in awe that I have done it. I could never have written it without you and Rochester. Thank you for helping me through all these present trials and hurts. I love You, dear Christ.

MONDAY, AUGUST 16, 1999

Incredible news!!!

This morning I received a call from Paul and he is excited about my book *The Enchantment of Writing.* I only sent it in July 28th—in fact writing about it was the last entry I made in this journal until this moment. Thank you, thank you, Jesus! Thank you, thank you, Paul! *Enchantment* is accepted! And I was the only one to read it before it was accepted! Thank you for showing me to have more confidence in myself. It was accepted in three weeks! Thank you!!!!

The next entry in this journal is not until December 23rd. It was a very unusual year and I just did not write in the journal from August until December, though I was doing much other writing and also writing in my Rochester Chronicle copy book and my steno pads as always.

THURSDAY, DECEMBER 23, 1999

Today is my birthday. I cannot believe it—it came around again so fast! I cannot believe how I can be this age... I am not going to write it now. I am not going to let it affect me. It is only a number. I feel I have been good about this all along. Bob had his birthday too, of course, on December 7th—Pearl Harbor Day. Birthdays have never brought me down because I know how young I feel and think and act. I hope my family does not think of me as old. I do not think Barb does. And I had June when I was very young. Oh well, it does not matter. I am me and I know how I feel. And I will be writing all my life. (I already have been) I have so much in me to write. So happy birthday to me and I am still wrapping Christmas gifts and am having a nice day with Bob and Rochester. Rochester is ever with me. I am appreciative for the loving calls from the girls and George. Thank you, Jesus. And I am remembering my parents on this birthday.

CHRISTMAS EVE
FRIDAY, DECEMBER 24, 1999

Bob, Chester and I had a very lovely day here and then Bob and I went to 5 PM Christmas Eve Mass at St. Anthony's. Beautiful! It was filled with the songs of children. Packed church—not like the attendance on regular Sundays. The poinsettias were on the altar for my Mother and Dad, Uncle Elmer, Dad Kolb and Friar Francis. That is comforting. We had a nice evening at home together—we three. Tomorrow we will be alone together in the morning and go up to the Inn in early afternoon and celebrate Christmas there.

An aside—there is a drawing I made here at the lower half of the page of a back view of Rochester sitting surrounded by four thick books. The drawing is in black ink and colored in with pastel colored pencils. It is very sweet to me to honor Rochester. One book is titled Writing, *another* Journal, *the third* Art *and the fourth* Poetry. *They speak of my interests. Rochester is my Angel and over them all.*

A section of the church program is glued in on the next page and we were pleased the names we always submit for poinsettias were at the top of the very long list. A "first" that they were at the top. It is so moving to see their names.

CHRISTMAS DAY
DECEMBER 25, 1999

We had a beautiful Christmas—a day to remember. We were alone together we three in the morning and up at the Inn we had another wonderful Christmas with Jessica, Michael, Maxine, Renee and Clayton. The entire day was perfect and lovely. Bob and I knew what our gifts to each other would be because we talked about it ahead of time. We usually never do this—but each only needed one thing so decided to do this. Bob gave me a wonderful camera with a telescopic lens so that I can take close ups of birds and animals and insects in nature for my writing. I was going to buy it with my own money—part of the money earned from sales of my book *Higher Ground* at Bookland, but he wanted to buy it for me so that was nice. I bought him a chain saw then with part of that earned money—the gift he really wanted. It is even partly green—our favorite color. We also had our stocking gifts to each other and Chester which are fun. Up at the Inn we all loved each others gifts and the time spent together. We got home about 8:45 PM and had a nice rest of the evening here with Chester as always. Chester has his own stocking, a beautiful needlepoint one with a picture of a marmalade cat looking out a window and red velvet on the back. He always has little gifts in it. He is pure gift!

MY LITTLE ONE —

You have been here through the years—
You have been here through the tears—
You have always made me smile—
You have gone the extra mile.
Through every kind of weather—
We have always been together.
You are my shadow, my little love—
You are my Angel from above
Thank you God
For my beloved Rochester

For Rochester   Jan
My Angel   September 14, 1999

Glued on a page alone is a picture of our entire immediate family, Bob, myself and six children in 1970: Janna just a baby. Santa is in the picture also with Jessica on his knee. It is taken in our living room. Santa was a close friend who came to the door that night and surprised all our children. We used it as a Christmas Card Bob made along with the picture of Matilda the Moose and a poem I wrote about her called "Magical Addition." It is glued in this journal five pages forward from this page.

WEDNESDAY, JANUARY 26, 2000

A NEW LIFE

Born today at 4:33 PM—is a baby boy to Dennis and Patti—
and a brother to Sarah and Jenny.
Announcing: Michael Patrick Clancy
                     11 lbs., 5 oz.—23 inches
                     Welcome, dear little one!
                     We love you sight unseen.

SUNDAY, MARCH 12, 2000

The days go by and I do not write in here even though I want to write. I add poems and pictures but I do not write. There is so much to write that it sort of overwhelms me because I have gotten behind and I do not write in here at all even though I am doing much writing on a new book. This weekend has been filled with snow, surely eight inches or more, more I am certain. It began yesterday around noon and was ending when we woke. Bob had put the car at the top of the hill before it got too bad. We could not go to church this morning and held our own Church Service using our own book *Whispered Notes* for the meditation and music and discussed the message and much more. These personal home services are really inspiring to us both. We have had two beautiful days though snowed in and I have gotten so much thinking done in regard to the book I am writing and so much writing and reading, that it is great!

Bob, too, has been trying to figure out the music program so he can use it to complete the hymn he wrote at my request for my latest book on writing (*The Enchantment of Writing*). This program has been difficult for him but he finally has it figured. But despite our separate work the three of us (Chester too) have spent a lot of time together and also he is looking at the basketball games he loves.

There are so many things I should have recorded in here but I cannot now and am not going to worry or berate myself about it as I do about a lot of things. I was doing other worthwhile writing, so that's that!

Even now there is other writing I want to get done today so I am not going to linger in here. I just wanted to touch base in these pages and break the cycle of not writing in here hoping that will now draw me back more faithfully to writing in here.

In Tibetan Buddhist culture, prayer flags "confide spiritual longings to the winds." As the small flags are gradually worn away by the elements, the prayers are believed to disperse throughout the universe.

I love it when I do write in here. I love writing so much. But I just cannot do every kind of writing I want to and my journal writing has suffered. Plus so many things have happened that kind of threw me for a loop and I just did not want to write about them and I still may not. But I get absolute blocks because of things like that because I do not want to relive them by writing about them. I will stop now. Rochester has been with me here as always. He is my dear little beloved. It is appropriate a quote about snow is below, entered in here previously, since we are snowed in as I write. I will stop now so we three can have a nice evening together. It has been a lovely day. Everything outside looks so beautiful and I thank God this is our home.

> *A heavy snowfall disappears*
> *into the sea. What silence!*

—Zen saying

Often the really important events are silent.

SIMPLE WEALTH

You've doubled the thick comforter
    once, twice.
        Oh, that's nice!
Ascending the layers of four—
    I gently pour
        my limber self
            onto the soft folds.
    Such simple wealth!
        It holds me
            in the deep.
                Ah, now to sleep.

Written for   Jan
Rochester   October 4, 1999
With deep love —   Feast of St. Francis of Assisi
(as he naps on the bed next to my desk)

STARS

I look up at the heavens
    and see the stars—
        like millions of twinkling eyes.
I am overwhelmed by their beauty,
    their serenity.
        Nothing mars
            the velvet blanket
                of the night skies.

I have no identity
    lost beneath this vast array,
        a mere speck—
            covered by celestial display.

Dedicated to	Jan
the night skies	October 5, 1999
of New Hampshire	

TUESDAY, APRIL 25, 2000

The hardest years in life are those between ten and seventy.

—Helen Hayes

It is a beautiful day but very cool, after many days of rain. It even rained all day Easter as we travelled down to Rhode Island and back to be with George, Val, Janna, Bill and all the children. But Good Friday and Saturday it snowed! Unbelievable, so late in April! I cannot write here now because I am working on my book, but I just wanted to make an entry because it had been so long. I am writing in another journal too though, given to me by Don Richards at Christmas. It is very unusual and I will mention it soon again. My beloved Rochester is right here with me on his quilt as I write. At this rate I am never going to finish this journal. I write so much when I am working on a book that I fail in this journal keeping.

THURSDAY, MAY 25, 2000

A lot has taken place in this last month and I am still not good about writing in here, but I am doing so much other writing on my book, plus am still using the other journal I mentioned in the previous journal entry. I have to get back to writing on my book *Beneath the Stars and Trees*. I get sick of worrying and being stressed. It is so calming to work on this book.

Those who love you and were helped by you will remember you.
So carve your name on hearts and not on marble."

—C.H. Sprugeon

MAGICAL ADDITION

When we drew open the curtain
          just after dawn—
We knew then for certain
          there was a moose on our lawn.
Exchanging glances
          with two humans that day—
She delighted in the circumstances,
          and decided to stay.
What a magical addition
          this enormous recluse!
So we began the tradition—
          to entertain moose.

                    Jan
                    November 1, 1999

Have a wonderful and joyous Christmas. Bob, Jan—and Rochester

The first poem I wrote about Matilda. We are putting it in our Christmas Card. (the card is a picture of her) and Bob added the small picture on top of the poem of her as seen here.

When tears come,
I breathe deeply and rest.
I know I am swimming
in a hallowed stream
Where many have gone before.
                    —Mary Margaret Frank in *Thoughts Matter:*
                    The Practice of Spiritual Life

It goes on to say in the poem that "my heart is at work" and "my soul is awake."

We should explore what our heart and soul is telling us through our tears the next time we cry.

We are doing great with our new bookstore and sold five books just since last night. Will write more about that too—and the book I am writing.

EPIPHANY
JANUARY 6, 2001

So much has happened since last I wrote in this journal eight months ago. I was writing in another journal and completed that. More recently I have been more scattered and have not written in a journal. This journal spans such a long time. I never meant it to be this way and perhaps I should not complete it. It has a lot of sadness in it too, and since writing in it last, I have completed a book titled *Beneath the Stars and Trees— There is a Place.* I will write about it another time. It was therapy for me to write it and I think it is such a beautiful book.

My beloved Rochester is here with me in my writing room as I write all cuddled in his blanket on the bed. He had been on my lap first. It is so comforting to have his continual blessed presence. He is my precious love. (There is a sweet picture of him on this page also.)

I chose to write on Epiphany because I have had an epiphany and I am not the same as I used to be when last I wrote in this journal. I will write more later, but I wanted to enter that on this day of Epiphany.

MONDAY, JANUARY 8, 2001

Yesterday was Epiphany in the church—on our wedding anniversary! That was lovely and we had a lovely anniversary beginning with going to Mass and then to breakfast at the Miss Wakefield Diner. We also celebrated when we went to Sanford, Maine on Friday for our usual excursions and errands, and had dinner at Shains. Delicious!

It is just too difficult to write about many of the things that occurred since last I wrote. Rochester is with me always. How I love him.

TUESDAY, JANUARY 9, 2001

I have gotten some wonderful reviews for my *Journal of Love* and that makes me so happy. That book means so much to me and to Rochester.

I have not written a poem in so long. It has been the strangest period. I want to get back to work on the book I started. I thought I would today, but I had so many things to mail out that I could not. Tomorrow.

My beloved Rochester is here with me now as always. I will close and the three of us will begin our evening. Perhaps I will write in here tomorrow, but then again, maybe not.

WINTER'S PLAY

I put you out to play today—
> your many arms now swing and sway,
While each and every fuchsia flower —
> in dance, can feel its inner power.
And as prevailing breezes stream—
> to move you as you sit and dream—
Your pot with flower fairy face,
> adds to this scene of joy and grace.

Dedicated to   Jan
"Winter"   November 3, 1999
my lovely Christmas Cactus at play,
on a warm November day

ROCKS

These silent witnesses
> to all that has passed before—
> > hold secrets deep within.
For those that behold them now
> they are vaults of knowledge
> > waiting to be tapped—
> > > waiting for one who will listen
> > to the whispers
> > > from these ancient beings.

Jan
November 23, 1999

Betrayal

Betrayal is like a knife in the heart,
and though it is resisted —
right from the start,
it is turned and twisted—
slaying the spirit.
I fear it.

Jan
November 24, 1999

Even a small star shines in the darkness.

—Finnish proverb

My Rochester is always my shining star. Always.

Never a day passes but that I do myself the honor to commune with some of nature's varied forms.

—George Washington Carver

George Washington Carver's life and his work and writings are important to me. I have written of him in my *Journal of Love* and first came to know about him as a young child. His life and words have helped me on my journey to experience nature more deeply and in my communication with nature and Rochester and God's creatures.

Oh how I love and experience Rochester and there is a divine and spiritual communication.

WEDNESDAY, JANUARY 10, 2001

Here I am writing in here again and I still really do not want to be. I cannot find a journal I began in Fall before everything happened to me, so I continue in here until I do, I guess. I am still inundated in mail and cards to answer and it overwhelms me. But they are from kind people: friends, family, acquaintances, and we exchange through the years. I got some of the answers done earlier today. Each one took time but they are worthy (the people—and the letters). I also want to be writing on a book as always.

I cannot stop thinking about a book I read by Clare Sylvia called *A Change of Heart*. Bob is reading it now at my request which is unusual because he very rarely reads a book that I do. (We read in entirely different genres.) So I am appreciative. I wanted us to be able to discuss it.

I asked Bob to order several copies of it so I can give it to others and he ordered it on the Internet. He was able to get expensive hardback copies of it for a much, much lower price. My copy is paperback so I will keep a hardback. This one has her picture on. I had bought my paperback in Bookland. I will read it again in hardback. I gave a new paperback to Ginny for Christmas before knowing about these hardbacks.

Rochester is on his quilt here asleep as I write. I will stop writing now here and get to work on my other writing.

Close Encounter with a Moose

She is chomping branches—
    and as I move in quietly,
        she compliantly
            allows my presence—
                with occasional glances
                    at this stranger.
As I gaze at the eloquence
    of this massive creature—
        and speak to her gently,
            I sense no danger.
I am a beseecher
    on behalf of the human race,
        as I intently
            speak love in this quiet place;
Revealing my respect—
    yearning to protect—
        seeking to connect
            with this wondrous teacher.

For Matilda   Jan
Moose of our Woods   November 10, 1999

Our bookstore is doing great and we regularly continue to get orders. I enjoy doing this (the bookshop) and really love our name too: "The Enchanted Forest Bookshop." Sent out several orders earlier today. I put little personal notes on pretty small paper to the people and always use my rubber stamp on the bottom that is of a lovely marmalade cat (I use a light brown ink pad and it gives that effect) symbolizing Rochester. He is part of our bookshop.

JANUARY 18, 2001

Here I am again writing in here. Just today I finally found the other journal with the lovely lotus flowered cover (or Water Lilies) and my "Rochester Chronicle" copy book. They were together safely but I had not been able to find them in a couple of weeks.

Here is dear Matilda, (I am glad I gave her my mother's middle name. It is sweet.) (A picture of her is glued in.) I think of her every day and wish she would return to us. Under the picture is typed (by Bob) "Matilda—resident Moose at Higher Ground."

At least I have made her alive through my writing in my own book *Beneath the Stars and Trees* and in the story I wrote for author Brad Steiger that he requested.

IN THE LINKING OF OUR EYES

O great brown moose—
    a delight to the eyes,
        a wondrous surprise,
            roaming loose
                in the tangled woods.
Strong, slender legs
    that stomp and crush
        the underbrush
            so lovely and tall.
Dark chocolate moose—
    soulful, inquiring, inspiring,
        is the rare, gentle, sweetness of your stare.
            O, what human and creature could share
    if we only dare.

What are you thinking?
In the linking of our eyes lie
mysteries untold,
may they slowly unfold.
In these moments of silence—
is sensed a sacred, unspoken alliance.

For Matilda   Jan
the moose   November 12, 1999

I thank you, dear Christ, with all my heart for Bob's perfect appointments on Monday. I have thanked you many times already but I want to write it here.

I will write more about the appointments the next time I write in here. Thank you, dear Christ.

Small rocks near water are like children gathered round with arms outstretched toward the Mother rock. On a mountain there is a large rock, the elder, that seems to reach out and gather the children about him.
                                    —Lu ch'ai, Chinese painter

There is a sweet small picture glued in here of George's and Val's little twins that I took at the Inn New Year's Eve 2000. (Natalie Marie and Melia Barbara)

It is appropriate I should land on this page because I think I must look like this dear bird whose picture I have glued in at the bottom. I feel frustrated and feel like crying and like I believe this dear baby Heron is doing. (his picture shows him/her with wild eyes and his feathers or down all standing up and frazzled around and on top of his head. And his beak is wide open and he obviously is either crying out or waiting for his mother to feed him! Regardless—he looks like I feel. I want to help him. He is a baby Black Crowned Night Heron. I feel oppression from someone and I am helpless.

Blessed are the cracked, for they shall let in the light.
                                            —Unknown

Reflections by the Lake

until I had looked at the photo many times. There is a lace table on the table and a flowered rug I remember that is in both the living room and dining room. It all makes me sad. It was taken sometime in 50s, year not certain. I discovered the photo while getting pictures together to put in my book *The Enchantment of Writing*. Here is a picture of our Christmas Tree in our living room here in cottage on the next page taken December 1999.

Life's journey is circular it appears. The years don't carry us away from our fathers—they return us to them.
                                                    —Michael Marriott

We went to Mass and afterwards at Close to Home. A nice morning together. I offered everything up at Mass that is concerning me and also thanked Jesus in deepest gratitude for being free of my asthma and other blessings. It is 7 PM and Bob was watching a game and I was reading and writing with Rochester. Isabelle is here too and enjoying her time here. She is such a good and sweet dog. Our Sunday is so different than our weekdays.

Our bookstore continues to do great and we get nice ratings. Sold three books in one day this week and others beside. I enjoy taking care of them, writing nice notes to enclose in each and gift wrapping each book.

Gratitude is the memory of the heart.
                                                    —Massieu

I gave Clara a book on Reiki yesterday because she has been learning the practice. I have a fine book on the subject too, given to me by Joanne Clancy, who is a Reiki Master. I ask the Holy Spirit to bless my hands because she used Reiki at a distance for me after I called her and asked her to pray for a concern.

The photo on the previous page of our cottage with the Christmas lights on cottage and tree in the snow taken in February last year is so similar to today and the glorious way it looks outdoors, except it is even deeper today—much deeper!

I am trying to write a book on all forms of prayer but I cannot because I feel this way. I have to try and rise above it all and get back to being strict about writing as I usually am. My spirit is broken.

AWAITED BIRTH

What is this poem within me now—
That longs to surface—and somehow—
I feel it pressing for release,
It will not rest nor give me peace.
Break forth and let yourself be known—
That I may let your utterances be shown.
And I shall write you word by word—
And permit your message to be heard.
Come now—it's far past your gestation
Please grant me a shred of illumination.

Dedicated to Poetry   Jan
                                             November 24, 1999

And did you get what
you wanted from this life, even so?
I did.
And what did you want?
To call myself beloved, to feel myself
beloved on the earth.
                        —Raymond Carver, "Late Fragment" from
                        A New Path to the Waterfall (Atlantic Monthly Press, 1989)

This poem was written by Raymond Carver when he was dying of cancer. It is in Natalie Goldberg's book *Long Quiet Highway* that I have just completed reading—either the third or fourth time—a book that has great meaning to me.

This poem makes me cry. It is so beautiful this writer felt "beloved on this earth" before he died. I do not feel beloved now and never will. How precious it must be to be beloved. Am I to Bob? I am to Rochester and he is to me. How precious I am beloved to Rochester and he to me.

There is so much sadness in this journal. This has been the strangest Fall and Winter. Help us dear Christ now to go on and experience great joy with our lives, Bob, Rochester and myself. This is our dream.

PRIMITIVE WRITING

Rocks are like primitive writing—
    meant to be held and read—
        examined with care and prayer.
          Their mere presence is inviting.
The crannies, hues and markings shed
    wisdom and light on a midnight thoroughfare
      to the inner unknown.
        Befriend a stone!

                Jan
                November 30, 1999

MELANCHOLIA

I am melancholia.
    In a stream of dispiritedness
      I encircle the heart—
        injecting it
          with dejection,
            and comfortlessness—
              until it sinks.

In a rush of darkness
    ascending to the mind—
      saturating it with disconsolateness
        dashing its spirit,
          dampening its hope,
            preying on whatever shred
              of light remains
                until it shrinks—
I take leave—
    knowing I have done my job.
      Inconsolable, sad, in reprieve,
        I sob.

                Jan
                December 3, 1999

This poem was written on my mother nothing to do with her, but everything to d penings in the summer of 1999.

The pen is the tool of the i
It may take you places you never though

S

REMEMBERING

For twenty-one years
    I could not celebrate
      your birthday
        as before.
But through the tears
    I never forget the date—
      and want to say
        once more—
Happy Birthday, Mother.
  I love you.

For Violet M. Gray
My Mother
Entered Heaven
September 26, 1978

Jan
Decem

I thought this photo on the opposite page (there is a co glued in) very nice to put with this poem. It is a picture of our at 6231 N. Third Street, Philadelphia, PA 19120 where I liv parents and grew up. It is decorated for Christmas with card hanging over the wide open doorway area that is between the liv and dining room. The Christmas cards are hanging over the poinsettia is sitting on the coffee table in front of the sofa in th room. My framed high school graduation picture is on the mant to other poinsettias over the artificial stone fireplace. There are an and coals in the fireplace that can be lit by electricity to look rea Mother is sitting at the dining room table in the semi-dark and I di

see her
cover
ing ro
the 19
togeth

our c

tog
th
bl
w
S
w

I have decided to complete this journal even though there is so much in it from the past. It deserves completion. It is a very significant journal actually of my past—and now my present. The poems are extremely important and significant.

PRAYER FOR DINLESSNESS

I try to sleep—
        but my thoughts are aisled
            to memory defiled—
                by things present—
                    things past—
                        I am wild—
                            within.

Please help me find
        peace of mind.
            Explode this din—
                I am your child.

                        Jan
                        December 11, 1999

WHEN I AM SAD

I write me a poem
        when I am sad,
            and my heart
                watches the words appear—
                    through the glistening tear
                        in my eye.
And when I am finished
        and the sadness diminished
            I am glad.
                I go apart
                    and sigh.
Reading the words that flew out—
        tells me what I'm about—
            and why.

Writing steals sadness —
    drives away madness—
      and heals.

Jan
December 29, 1999

Each organ in Chinese Medicine interconnects with an emotion.
Sadness belongs to the lung.

A very long poem is entered here written to Bob and dated December 16, 1999, too personal to include, discussing a deep sadness and trauma—but ending in a joy and hope of all the previous pain being banished forever and love allowed to reign and remain.

WRITTEN DECEMBER 16, 1999

I pray on Bob and Rochester. I do "laying on of hands" on Rochester every day. He is so dear and affectionate—my Star, my sunshine, my precious one.

MONDAY, FEBRUARY 5, 2001

Good morning, dear Christ and my Angels. And dear Mary. I am not going to write in here at length but spend the day writing otherwise.

6:30 PM

A snow storm began in early afternoon and is supposed to be 12 inches. It is beautiful though. I am at my desk with the porch light on and can see all the lovely snow coming down outside. So magical.

AT LAST

Today—twenty-one years later
    on your birthday—
I think of you lying in your coffin
    in your pretty dress of black and gray,
Worn at your husband's and brother's funerals
    when they had gone so quickly away
      in that three month period in nineteen seventy seven.

And though you are in Heaven
    free of your shoes and earthly ties—
I cannot bear to think of your body
    lying there in that coffin in heels.
        I hear your sighs.
And too, I hear your words from the coffin—
    "Take off my shoes!"
        and I understand.

Though you wore heels day in and day out
    and all about at work—
        and looked so grand—
The moment you came home
    you kicked off your shoes
        and slipped into your slippers.
You even served us your finest meals
    while wearing slippers!
        How did I—in nineteen seventy eight—not remember?
But I do now this day in December!

In tears at your leaving
    my sadness overwhelming—
        I did not think to remove
            each heel.
        Then came the seal!
O, how did you endure for twenty-one years
    what you could not even for a moment
        when you arrived home?
            You must have been in tears!

Please put my heart and yours at rest—
    and though it will take weeks—your body being dead—
Gently lift your thin left leg and with your small foot
    push off your right shoe—
Now, very slowly—lift your bare right foot
    and push off the last heel.
        Oh, how does that feel?

Just let those heels fall where they may!
 Your feet—at last—are at rest today!
  O, if only I could give you your slippers—
   but I am four hundred and twenty miles away.

For Violet M. Gray—my mother   Jan
Happy Birthday   December 3, 1999
with my love

TUESDAY, FEBRUARY 6, 2001

When I work, I leave my body outside the door, the way the Moslems take off their shoes before they enter a mosque.
—Pablo Picasso

This day has been lovely spent with Rochester upstairs here in our writing room and the glorious scenery outside. The snow storm went all night. We got close to 24 inches! We were ploughed in the morning. Later we were able to go to the Post Office. Received a very unusual letter from Joanne (Clancy) in response to some gifts I gave to her and the letter really blesses me and in part concerns Rochester. Will write about it another time. It is about six typed pages and I have read it twice already. She also wants to share something else when she used Reiki at a distance for me after I called her and asked her to pray when I went in for my procedure.

The picture on the previous page of our cottage in the snow taken in February last year is so similar to today and the way it looks except it is even deeper today—much deeper!

I have decided to complete this journal even though there is so much in it from the past. It deserves completion. It is a very significant journal actually, of my past, and now my present. The poems are extremely important and deeply significant.

A long poem is entered here that is too personal to include now.

I still do not have to use my regular inhaler during the day or night or any time at all. It is a true miracle! I have even gone to the Post Office two days without my inhaler when normally I always have it in my pocket. It is by the bed these last two days. I use only the two inhalers morning and night he prescribed and let them stay by the bed too—two puffs on each. After that I NEVER need an inhaler again until twelve hours later. And I really do NOT need it or have any shortness of breath AT ALL! I use them twelve hours later only because that is what the doctor told me to do! I will be seeing him tomorrow and cannot wait to tell him what a difference he has made in my life. I feel brighter, I think I look better, and I have more energy. It is so amazing not to be using that inhaler every three hours and often it was less than that—I mean less than three hours and more frequent. It was particularly hard getting ready to go out early anywhere, like to church. This past Sunday it was a breeze. I was out of here in a flash! It really is all a miracle.

A wise man feels he is not so wise, otherwise, he is not wise.
—Fred VanAmburgh

Today is Ronald Reagan's 90th birthday. it seems impossible this could be so. He is a good man and I am so sorry he has Alzheimer's. It is terrible. He and his wife Nancy seem devoted. Recently he broke his hip but he is doing well and they say he is vigorous and strong and should live many years. He and Nancy have been married for 48 years—a very long time.

IT TAKES TIME

One can die of a broken heart.
　　You slip and slide downward
　　　　into the mire—
　　　　　　a quicksand pulling
　　　　　　　　you deeper and deeper
　　　　　　　　　　into sadness and despair.
There is nothing to cling to—
　　　　yet you reach out to grasp
　　　　　　again and again.
　　　　　　　　Your heart splits in two
　　　　　　　　　　and you submerge into the depths—
　　　　　　　　　　　　arms and hands upright
　　　　　　　　　　　　　　trying to cling to Heaven
　　　　　　　　　　　　　　　　to help you.

But you sink and sink—
 your own tears adding to
  all that surrounds you—
   all that pulls you down—
    and then you are gone
     into the unfathomable
      abyss.
One day you shall rise again—
 but it takes time.

             Jan

WEDNESDAY, FEBRUARY 7, 2001

It is a beautiful cold sunny day and is now 4:10 PM. I mailed Joanne (Clancy) a copy of Claire Sylvia's book—*A Change of Heart*. I want her to have it. Will discuss it all more later and Joanne's letter.

I forgot to mention that recently when in Wolfeboro and to the Health Food Store for brown rice and other items, I stopped in my favorite store "Made on Earth" before we left Wolfeboro and that is always uplifting to do. Got a new book. Will write about it another time. It is titled *Finding My Fables* by Gaylyn Britton. I was going to buy it other times when I was in but never did. Decided I was to do it today. That store is so incredible—so many spiritual books and statues and religious items and statuary carved from wood, and jewelry. It makes me happy when I go in there but I stay in the book section with only a few glimpses elsewhere right before I leave. I love that this store is selling my book *Compassion for All Creatures* on their shelves. The cover is so beautiful with my little beloved's face on the cover. How I love him. My book had been in their store window for a long period too.

Rochester is here with me in our writing room looking so precious in his big wildlife quilt asleep. I am so blessed by his love and presence. Isabelle is still with us and she is downstairs watching birds out the front sliding windows seated in the corner of the sofa with her sweet curly head resting on the sofa back as she enjoys the wildlife. Bob just went over to the Birchgrove.

A METAPHOR

Snow—a metaphor for life—
    arrives in all its innocent beauty
       from the heavens,
          magnificent and pure.—
            slowly fades —
              disappears
                into
                  the
                    earth.

Like life—
    its essence
      is drawn to the Sun—
        absorbed into Him.

            Jan
            March 2000

LATER

We talked to Jessica quite a while earlier and she is getting weary without Michael here. He and Maxine will return from Russia with their church group and she will meet him late at night in Boston. Her friend Laura is taking her. Bob and I volunteered also. It has seemed long for her to be apart from Michael but Bob and I were talking about this and he and I were apart for six long months while he went overseas, and four of those months I had infant June with me and he did not see her until she was 4 months old. None of my children ever had such an experience of being separated from their spouses like that—plus giving birth without the support of a spouse. Without my parents helping it would have been so hard for me and baby June.

I will be glad when Michael and Maxine are safely home with Jess and Renee and Clayton. I am so happy they had the experience of Russia—but I will just feel better when that little family is all back together again in the Inn. Oceans are too big to be between those who love.

When God measures a man, He puts the tape around the heart instead of the head.

—Anonymous

There is a picture I glued in at the bottom of the page of a lovely Irish green beaded Rosary.

My beloved little Rochester is right here by me on the quilt on the bed and he gives me such joy I will close on that note and continue with my other writing.

(A picture of Rochester and our Christmas tree taken early in January 2001 is on the next page.)

FRIDAY, FEBRUARY 9, 2001

On the next five or six pages in my journal I recorded about a person who stalked me for quite a few years. Because there were three new phonecalls in one week and a persistence in wanting to come to New Hampshire to visit me and to stay at the Inn as well, I felt it necessary to record everything. It began in the early 1990s when we lived in Jenkintown. We had to change our phone system here in New Hampshire after the numerous new contacts. This all seemingly began when the person learned about my first published book and it revolved around some of the others that followed.

I cannot write it all out as I have in this journal for it is so personal. There were numerous factors involved. It lasted several more years about 15 years total, till sometime in 2005, then an unusual thing occurred in this person's life that truly showed we were correct in our summation of it all and that indeed, the person was deeply troubled and ill. There has been no further contact, but I do keep the person in my prayers.

7:15 PM

Last night in the middle of the night I was led to open a book I have had by my bed for many many months. I had finished reading a book by Melody Beattie and laid it aside (it was excellent) and picked up this other book titled *Awakening Intuition—Using your Mind —Body Network for Insight and Healing* by Mona Lisa Schulz. I opened it at random and what I read was incredulous and made me cry. There on the page was the explanation of what happened to me and my heart that I had been trying to explain to Bob and my children and my doctors. I was stunned that what I knew I had experienced was a true phenomenon! I had told my Doctors and they listened and knew I was sincere in my beliefs. But I had no one to back me up or no writings about it. Now here in this book is exactly what I was telling them that I knew was what happened to me. Oh thank you dear Christ and my Angels for allowing me to open this rather thick book—and have my eyes fall on the very paragraph that explains what happened to me and to my heart. It is an absolute miracle it should be there and I open to the very place! Now at least I have medical backing and explanation for what I have been trying to explain. I will copy it out and I already have copied it into another journal—a journal I began only two days ago (February 8) to write about what happened to me in November and to help me remember forgotten things about it. Thank you, dear Christ!

And so at last this journal comes to an end in a joyful way for it is filled with my sadness. I am glad I completed it. I think it deserved that. I am glad so many of these things are behind me now. Thank you, dear Christ for your healing.

On last inner plain page written about this journal:

DECEMBER 1999

To write a book
    is to bare your heart
        upon a page.
            I'm no wise sage—
                but I've done my part —
                    but please don't look.

                      —Jan

Jessica and Michael Drakely in the Hitching Post Village Inn in Center Ossipee, New Hampshire

MEDITATION SEVEN

The Journals of
Cecily Mary Barker

*I have had many more mysterious encounters which cannot be
easily explained. These lead me to believe that fairies really do exist.*
—Cicely Mary Barker, 14 September 1930,
from a personal letter to her friend Dulcie
in *How to Find a Flower Fairy*

YEARS AGO in the Renaissance Card Company's beautiful and intriguing gift shop that is an important part of their company and building
in Sanford, Maine, I discovered the *Flower Fairies* by Cicely Mary Barker.
These lovely Fairies appeared on a large selection of the Renaissance
Greeting Cards and once I did discover them I bought the greeting
cards to send to friends and relatives each time I visited this wonderful
store. They also carried large and small books about the Flower Fairies
and frequently I would also buy one or two of the 4x6 hardback books
each with a lovely glossy paper jacket cover on which appeared a Flower
Fairy. The hardback cover itself was identical to the glossy paper cover
with picture that protected it. Within the pages were beautiful colorful
prints of the Flower Fairies, but with only one Fairy in each painting in
a natural setting with trees or flowers. The art work is so delicate and
lovely but opposite each colored piece of art is a lovely poem about each
Flower Fairy written by the artist Cicely. The books are all a joy to behold
and own and appreciate, and too, to give as gifts. They easily became
collectors items. I have this series of eight books and have enjoyed them
for years now. *They are the Flower Fairies of the Spring, the Summer, the
Autumn, the Winter, of the Trees, of the Garden, of the Wayside and of the
Alphabet.* Guests too that used to stay in my writing/prayer room over

164

night always seemed to enjoy these books as well as finding other books to get involved in. The *Flower Fairies* are enchantment and beauty.

These *Flower Fairy* books are published by Frederick Warne and the Penguin Group of publishers. There are many other books by Cecily I have never seen such as *The Lord of the Rushie River* and *Simon the Swan*. Her little poems are as lovely as her delicate paintings.

The original editions of the *Flower Fairy* books were first published in the 1920s and the beautiful new editions were designed to recapture the charm of these originals. I feel fortunate to have discovered them. It is stated on each jacket cover that Frederick Warne has been able to achieve reproductions of Cecily Mary Barker's original artwork by using modern printing techniques which reflect better than ever before her outstanding craftsmanship as an artist.

A new generation of readers will be enchanted by Cecily's delicate brushwork, detail and subtle shadings.

It is written that Cicely was born in Croydon, South London in 1895 and died in 1973 and that she was always happiest with a sketchbook in her hand. Because of her ill health she was educated at home and largely taught herself to draw and paint. When she was only 15 years old and despite her formal artistic training, her natural talent was commercially recognized with the publication of a set of postcards.

But in 1923 it was her *Flower Fairy* books, her first published that year, that brought her international acclaim as an artist. It is stated in each flyleaf of her covers that it was the delicate charm of her illustrations, coupled with her meticulous botanical accuracy, that has caused her books to become classics of children's literature, and these books have captivated both children and adults alike for nearly 70 years. I particularly enjoy the varied forms in which her poetry is written. Imagine having the artistry and talent for both delicate art work and the writing of poems!

With all of this background of Cicely being shared you can then possibly understand how surprised and delighted I am upon receiving two very unique gifts as if from another world by our daughter Laurel and husband Richard.

The first gift of an amazing large book, 9x12 in size in hardback, but with soft padded covers, arrived for my birthday in December. The cover is a beautiful violet or lavender with fairies, flowers and vines down the sides of the binding and around the edges. Violet is one of my favorite colors as well as green. There is a lovely flower in a three dimensional framed oval on the top center that changes and reveals a fairy hidden in it when you shift the position of the book. The title beneath it reads *Fairyopolis*—and in small script beneath A *Flower Fairies Journal.* Never have I seen such a journal and that is why I need to write of it for you. A smaller clear oval, but raised higher dimensionally than the other, is on the right middle end of the cover with delicate flower drawings around it. A close up of a pretty fairy with sweet child-like features is in the raised crystal. This oval and the art work around it give the appearance of a lock on the book itself.

Within the pages you find yourself in a land of enchantment. The first handwriting is on the inside cover and it is a copy of a letter from the author and artist Cicely dated 6th January 1923 in her handwriting to the British Fairie Folklore Society in Brighton Sussex. Among other words of introduction she writes: "I am sending the society a journal kept during the summer of 1920, when I felt particularly inspired to write and sketch copiously." She tells them she is entrusting her journal to them and is trusting them to preserve and look after her book and refers to them as "fellow Fairy Lovers."

Her handwriting is delicate, straight and small in the letter and throughout her journal. She is entrusting her journal to another just as I am entrusting my journals within this volume to my own publisher whom I trust.

On the inside page opposite this reproduction of her letter there is full length actual photo of the artist and author in a white dress and straw hat in front of a tree. It is clipped there with a paper clip (one that is sketched but seems real, for the photo can be lifted partially from the bottom). This overlaps a small left side portion of a bookplate that reads:

This journal belongs
to:
Cicely Mary
Barker

She has written in her name, and a lavender flower is there and a fairy below it dressed in violet. It is impossible to adequately describe this journal so that you can fully understand its utter unusualness and beauty, and too, its otherworldliness.

The entire journal is dated with each entry and in her handwriting in black ink. (All my journals back to September 1989 are in green ink and all before that in blue ink. Ink color seems to seriously matter to journal keepers and those who write much [letters, cards, books, etc.] The color is usually chosen for a reason—although perhaps back in the early 1920s only black ink was available. I would not know this for I would not yet be born for long time and I unfortunately have no precious family keepsake letters from that much earlier era.)

Throughout this journal it is not only otherworldly but other dimensional—in the sense of raised pictures, letters, and folders and envelopes that open, and a small Fairy Book of *Tales of Grateful and Helpful Fairies* that also opens with several pages and pictures within. The envelopes contain little notes and treasures you can pull out to examine and then return to the safety of the envelopes. A note next to one envelope states in Cecily's writing with an arrow pointing to it—"I believe this to be fairy dust." She states she is not imagining things and is relieved to at last find physical evidence of it.

The pages are interrupted so incredibly with her art work down the sides or in the middle of the writing, beautiful colors, fairies everywhere including actual drawings of several of her flower fairies that I have on note cards and on her small books. It truly is impossible to describe the many things she has put all over the pages in written and art forms. I still have never read it entirely through at one sitting for to do so would almost be wrong for you could not possibly see every little remark, journal entry or drawing and sketch! On the last inside back cover illustrated with many fairies and flowers is a lovely 4x6 envelope lightly sealed. You can gently unseal it (and it can always be resealed) and take out a viewer that is meant to look through (I do) and view fairies. The heavy envelope is a pretty design matching the interior of the back cover. On the outside of the back violet cover is a young boy fairy figure sitting on top of a paper note seemingly pinned to the cover and it has a closing to the book that reads, "As dusk fell, there was a magical feel—etc."

I hope this description will entice you to investigate this journal for yourself even though my descriptions cannot possibly tell you its beauty. It is filled with enchantment—and while a child would enjoy it for the art, they definitely cannot truly appreciate it for all the written journal writing. I personally feel it is for adults and with an adult present to then possibly be shared with a child for the art and dimensional aspects. It is delicate in form also and a pure treasure and should be read with care and respect.

If all of this was not enough, a journal treasure, I receive a second one for Mother's Day this year in 2008 from Laurel and Richard. This one is the same size but with a lovely shade of green cover with branches of trees, mushrooms, butterflies and fairies upon it. It is titled *How to Find Flower Fairies*—with a subtitle of *Discover an Enchanted Fairy World*. There is an oval dimensional hologram on the cover, this one centered, that changes from a large knot hole in a tree with fern about it, to an elf peering out of the now opened knothole when you shift the position of the journal.

In the inside cover is again a handwritten letter from Cicely and this time it is to a friend named Dulcie and dated 14th September 1930, and from the same address as the previous letter. A marbleized open capped fountain pen lies by the letter. On the inner page opposite this is the lovely title on a cream paper with delicate branches on the side and the title reads as it does on the front cover but it also states beneath it:

Research conducted by
Cecily Mary Barker"

Beneath this information and as always in Cecily's handwriting in black ink it says, "My camera has allowed me to capture glimpses of fairies as they explore our world." The word "our" is underlined. Butterflies and leaves and flowers are everywhere and a boy winged fairy in green sits upon the sign bearing the title. Beneath this is a four page photograph album that can be enjoyed with various photos and writings beneath them. Inside the first page in the lower right corner is another small book titled *How to Spot a Tree Fairy* with instructions and drawings on its several pages. There is also a beautiful drawing of a Tree Fairy in the upper right corner pointing out delicate features about him and his surroundings. Cecily's journal writing abounds on these pages and all through the journal. This journal is different in that it has pop-out art that is so magnificent! These particular two joining pages have an entire section of tree branches that pop-out filled with leaves, acorns, and a secret fairy house inside well hidden. Other pages have an entire dimensional tree trunk and hidden crevices to explore and a tiny multiple page book plus journal entries by Cecily. Each page holds enchantment and surprises in delicate pop-out nature and fairy art with accompanying journal writing and small books and other treasures. All the pop-outs are things of nature where the fairies hide and dwell. Too, there are pictures of fairies in a three dimensional marsh with lovely water lilies. The inside cover contains another short letter from Cecily to her friend Dulcie and an actual replica of a front page of the newspaper *The Sussex Herald* dated October 8, 1930 with headline reporting of a controversy surrounding a local Fairy Photograph. The article is about Cecily and how it is understood that she has captured the images of a fairy on camera. It goes on to say how she is known for her delicate and tasteful paintings of Flower Fairies and is the author of several little books about them. It was also reported in the article that a renowned fairy authority and enthusiast at a special meeting of the British Fairie Folklore Society said, "I firmly believe in the existence of the fairy race," and she went on to say she believed in the genuineness of the photograph.

On the back inside cover opposite the letter and newspaper is a small box expanding dimensional camera with an approximate 4x4 inch screen depicting a fairy in a tree branch that changes position when you move the book cover. The interior of the cover is pale violet and on the lovely green back padded cover is a sweet girl fairy in green holding a note from Cecily with magnifying glass nearby and butterflies. She states, "I have discovered that there are five special places where fairies make their homes." She tells us that in these places "they are able to live in harmony with nature, safely hidden from human eyes...."

What descriptions I have given here from these magnificent hand-written journals with incomparable art cannot begin to tell you their true worth and beauty just for the eyes to enjoy, but there is wisdom in the journal writings to ponder and explore in our own heart and mind. I hope you will perhaps look for these journals by Cecily Mary Barker in your bookstore or on a bookstore on-line. Mine were sent to me on both occasions by Laurel and Richard from Barnes and Noble and they are forever keepsake journals that I continually enjoy. Journals come in many forms.

Our daughter Laurel enjoys creative art and writing, and recently presented me with a poem she wrote about my dad. Laurel was born on her Pop-Pop's June 2nd birthday. I share her poem now with you.

POP-POP

Pop-Pop was a gentle soul
Still waters deeply run
A quiet steadfast spirit
His eyes—a glint of fun

June second was our date of birth
though many years apart
Our cake and ice cream always shared
as love within our heart

There were no big activities
No fireworks to flare
His light was bright, but steady
for he was always there

He—constant, unconditional
a harbor in the gale
I never had to prove myself
to him—I couldn't fail

His lessons are enduring
I reach back through my life
and grab hold of his wisdom
to help in times of strife

For strength is oft times silent
It doesn't cause alarm
It cushions all who venture near
and keeps our hearts from harm

—Laurel Elizabeth Kuhl

MEDITATION EIGHT

Jameson Up North

JAMESON WROTE THIS JOURNAL ENTRY in his school class. Each paragraph was a page, five in all, and illustrated by him. I include the first picture only which cannot be seen here in its true colors. It depicts Jameson in their car with a family member heading north to our home on a lake in the woods of New Hampshire. He and his family come here very often throughout each year and that is a blessing.

Jameson is the oldest child of our son George and daughter (in-law) Valerie. He has twin sisters, Melia and Natalie, who will soon be eight years old, and a frisky little Pugle (combination Pug and Beagle) dog named Roxanne.

Jameson was just turning nine years old last Fall in 2007 when he wrote this journal entry in his class in Rumford, Rhode Island. The original entry is printed in his own handwriting. He likes to kayak and fish with his Dad and play ball with his family when he is here, and with his cousins. And he loves to eat yogurt! A supply is always on hand when he and his sisters arrive.

Jameson is very knowledgeable about all of God's creatures and we discuss them often, and he reads about them always when here from my animal books and at home from his.

This unique handwritten journal entry with art was a gift to Bob and me from a precious Grandson.

A JOURNAL ENTRY
WRITTEN BY
JAMESON RONALD KOLB
EARLY FALL 2007

171

Up North at the Lake

On the way to the lake, I look through the window and look at all the pines. I hear the wind whipping on the roof and I smell the tasty French fries in the car. I taste my cold juice box and feel the warm sun blazing on my face.

Up north at the lake, I am a loon. I have white dots with bright webbed feet. I dive under water and when I get tired, I sit on the green wooden dock.

Up north at the lake, I am a black bear. I have pitch black fur with a little stumpy tail. I sneak quietly though the woods and take a bath in the shimmery pond.

Up north at the lake, I am a beaver. As I swim through the water, I see lake trout and other fish. I hear my oar-like tail smacking the water. I smell sap and taste the splintery wood. I feel the smooth wood.

When it is time to go, I pack my bags. Then I look at the beautiful sunset. Next my dad hitches the yellow kayak on the car. And then we're

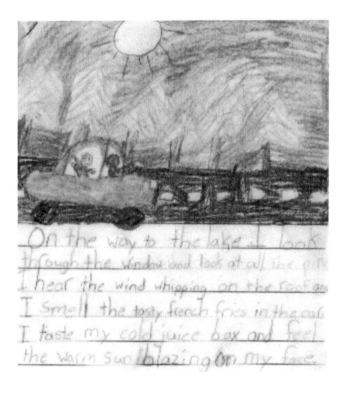

off. I shut my eyes tight and fix them in my mind. So when I am far away from New Hampshire, when I am home, I close my eyes and once again, I am up north at the lake.

Cousins
Two of the "October Boys"
left to right
Jameson Ronald Kolb
—author of this Journal Entry
age 9 years
and Clayton Walter Drakely
age 11 years
on "Higher Ground" by the lake—2007

MEDITATION NINE

My Musical Pictorial Journal

*Find a picture of yourself in early childhood and place it where
you will see it daily. Dialogue with the child in your picture.
Reflect upon the things you hear your child telling you in quiet times
and in prayer. Write all you receive into your journal.*
—Jan, *The Enchantment of Writing: Spiritual Healing
and Delight Through the Written Word*

In my possession for a number of years is a book titled *Anne Frank:
Beyond the Diary—A Photographic Remembrance* by Rund van der Rob
and Rian Verhoeven. If you have never read *The Diary of Anne Frank* that
I have written of previously in another meditation you may be moved to
do so eventually, but the book I have mentioned now at the beginning
of this meditation contains many photos of her diary pages, her family,
the hiding place and all else pertaining to Anne's life.

It is a true keepsake that I am thankful to own, along with several
copies of her diary I have had for years.

I speak of this pictorial journal because I have been blessed to receive
one of my own life this past Mother's Day created by our daughter Janna
and a gift from Janna and our son (in-law) Bill VanDorick and our grandchildren Dahlia, Cole and Rebecca. It was a true synchronism I should
receive this lovely journal and the Fairy Journals of Cicely Mary Barker
from daughter Laurel and son (in-law) Richard while actually writing
about and sharing my own personal journals in this book. They still do
not know I am writing about journals at this point in time.

*Janna and
Bill gave me
the Musical
Pictorial Journal*

The creation by Janna is not only pictorial however, but on a CD containing dozens of pictures accompanied by music of the big band sounds of the 40s and 50s era that Bob and I and friends totally enjoyed. Over a hundred pictures or more show the seriousness and total zaniness of all members of our family from the time our children were tiny through their marriages and all of their children at all ages. It is a true keepsake unlike anything I own.

I enjoyed creating many photo albums for my six children earlier in their lives, for my early life was not recorded in this way and there are very, very few photos of my childhood or teen years to be found. Janna begins the musical pictorial CD with the picture that will appear here in this meditation that was taken on the front lawn of our row home of 6231 N. Third Street on the outskirts of Philadelphia. I am guessing I am about three and a half to four years old.

I am so grateful for this gift of a "Journal" in musical pictorial form—a most unusual journal that is not the private sort I have been writing of or encouraging but one to be passed down to future family members. I have written in detail in my *Enchantment of Writing* about Photographic Journals but I had never created one with musical accompaniment though I was a creator of multiple photographic albums per child. They were not mere photo albums but had written stories about the photos accompanying them. These are totally unlike the written and very private journals I have been sharing and writing about in this book. I learned later Janna made too a CD of this same journal for herself and each of her four sisters and her brother. I am so appreciative for this gift—as is

Bob—that she gave of her time and talent and above all love—to create this
unusual photographic journal. Thank
you, dear Janna.

A poem I was inspired to write not
long after receiving this one-of-a-kind
personal musical journal of snapshots
tells of a brief "snapshot" moment in my
life when I was the age I am in this very
picture—the only difference being the
poem takes place in my back yard of our
row home and I am on the front lawn in
the picture.

SNAPSHOTS

Dotted Swiss curtains
Pretty as you please—
Kitchen window is open
They blow in the breeze.

Mother looks from the window
And calls love to me—
I am down in the yard
Happy and free.

A curly haired child
On a Summer day—
Daddy's cutting the grass
And I am at play.

So many years later
Memories I recall—
As with snapshots of old
I reflect on them all.

Jan
July 1, 2008

Woodland Colors

$\mathcal{T}$HE WRITINGS IN THIS JOURNAL are written within a magical cover of soft muted woodland colors with a border of gold and flowers. A young woman in a long gown lies asleep at the base of a tree amongst the ferns and she lies across both covers of the journal.

WEDNESDAY, MARCH 7, 2001

Life begets life
Energy creates energy.
It is by spending oneself
that one becomes rich.

—Sarah Bernhardt

And so I begin a new journal on this day in March at 4:40 PM. I am sitting at my desk in my Holy Writing Room and I dedicate this journal to Christ and my Angels and the Blessed Mother too—and always to my beloved Rochester who is here with me as always.

Sit in reverie and watch the changing color of the waves break upon the seashore of the mind.

—Henry Wadsworth Longfellow

You are a soul. Here is what you are and what these (your) episodes of writing are about.

There was a child went forth everyday,
And the first object he look'd upon, that object he became.

And that object became part of him for the day
or a certain part of the day.
Or for many years or stretching cycles of years. (Walt Whitman)

—from Richard Rhodes, *How to Write:*
Advice and Reflections

Writer Richard Rhodes states in his book following this poem (he also wrote the sentence preceding the poem):

No one makes craft carefully wrought, seem more casual than Walt Whitman. What your episodes are about is opening that fresh, innocent eye.

Rhodes is giving advice on writing using Whitman's poem. I have not copied out the next part that followed that he had in his book because it is quite long. It tells of all the things in nature and that Whitman met and saw that became a part of this child: the lilacs, grass, morning glories, song of the phoebe bird, lambs, and so much more.

I thought the two preceding pages would inspire me in the writing of my book because I have been having difficulty and it has only been coming through me slowly. I am attempting a book on prayer, many kinds of prayer, as I have mentioned in a previous journal.

The three childhood pictures of myself I have glued in the front of this journal are for a reason and I will explain later. Rochester's picture never needs a specific reason. He is my joy and love and inspiration. The book plate is symbolic of him too. I have been using these plates since Rochester was a kitten. They are by photographer Ron Kimball. (There are also bookmarkers with Rochester's "look alike" on too.)

MARCH 8, 2001

I had a very unusual dream right before I woke. Actually Bob woke me as he got up to put coffee on so it came to an abrupt end. But I tried to stay quiet with my eyes closed so I could still capture every detail of the dream, then I jotted it down briefly in my steno tablet. I lose so many dreams by being careless upon awakening, or I know I have been dreaming but cannot remember any of the dreams. So I am trying to be careful now. This was the dream.

There was a small group walking together. We seemed to be walking downward on a ramp in a concourse and we were coming to a turn. Bob was up ahead of us looking back as he was near the turn. I seemed to ask him if I could tell these people the news, and though I cannot remember me saying those words it was implied. He was laughing as he does. I sort of slowed the group down a bit. I was walking backwards talking softly to them and had my arms around two very heavy women facing them to tell them. One woman was black and one white. I was telling them that Father _____ was getting married. They asked his age and I told them his correct age. It seemed like they did not know him. I am only guessing. It was the impression I have. There was also talk about his dog, though I cannot remember the dog's name being mentioned. I somehow spoke about his dog at the end of the dream. We all had coats on so I guess it was colder weather like now. —End.

I received a most wonderful answer to prayer in the mail today. Cannot write of it now. Have to just ponder it all.

FRIDAY, MARCH 9, 2001

I had an 11 AM appointment with Dr. Fleet so he could find out how I was doing with the inhalers. I have not written about them in this journal but I will. No time now. The appointment went so well and I will write about all that transpired—but the amazing incredible outcome of it is that I do not have to go back to see him until November! That will be my yearly appointment! I am so thrilled and Bob is dumbfounded. I had an appointment in April but it was canceled. Thank you, thank you, dear Christ. Thank you!

We are going to the Poor Peoples Pub tonight for dinner to celebrate my new book *Beneath the Stars and Trees* and the contract that arrived Thursday the 8th for it from Blue Dolphin. We will celebrate this great news I received at my appointment too. I will write about it tomorrow or soon, now . Thank you, dear Christ and my Angels. And speaking of Angels, Rochester is right here with me now as always as I write.

Postscript: I add now in the present on May 30th, 2008 as I share this journal with you—that one year later on March 8, 2002—Rochester suddenly went to Heaven. It is always in the present moment as if it is just occurring. He passed away just as the manuscript was to be sent away to the printers and Paul (Blue Dolphin publisher) held the manuscript up so I could add a Memorial page for Rochester, my little Angel who had been my angel of inspiration and companion during the entire writing of this book, and each of my books. And in each book that followed Beneath the Stars and Trees *there is a Memorial Page to him and there always shall be.*

MONDAY, APRIL 2, 2001

I am so annoyed with myself that I let all this time pass since my last entry in here. I had such good intentions when I began this journal for writing in it regularly. I have been working on my new book and enjoying it very much—plus reading a lot, so this journal got neglected even though I carry it around the house with me with my steno pad and current book. From this notation forward I will try to do better, but will stop for now so I get back to work on my book about "prayer." Still no title for it. Rochester is here with me asleep on his quilt. How I love him. There are no words.

I will just quickly add, that on March 14th, Wednesday, I signed the contract from Blue Dolphin that I received in the mail March 8th (Thursday). We both had gone over it, then I signed and we mailed it. We then went to Maine for the day to do our usual day and errands and then had dinner at the diner and I felt like it was again a celebration of my book and the signing of the contract (for *Beneath the Stars and Trees— there is a place*). The poem that follows this entry is new that I wrote for the new book I am writing now.

And just another few lines to say we did have a nice time at the Pub that night (Friday, March 9). We had not been there in at least a year. We had delicious soup, homemade cream of tomato-like bisque and grilled cheese and tomato on rye. Not fancy, but good. Most of the meals have meat or fish so we are limited as to what we can eat.

> Poems happen in my life —
> making appearances—
> never interferences.
> They walk about at unsuspected times.
> And not in their soft soled shoes!

Often rhymes —
always lines—
fresh from within,
that I hear above the din
of my thoughts,
and I write them down.

I cannot lose
these messages
of God.

Jan
March 15, 2001

HOLY THURSDAY, APRIL 12, 2001

Spent today working on a chapter in my new book. the chapter is about making and creating our own prayer books. I have a lot of interesting things in it. I believe this then is the 11th chapter I have completed but they were not written in order. I wrote each one as I was led to write them. They are with Bob—all the completed chapters, waiting to be typed.

SATURDAY, MAY 5, 2001

I cannot believe that I have done it to myself again—that I have let all this time elapse without writing in here. I have been working on my book though. And also I was sent proof reading to do by Paul. But I want to write more and there is not time now. I just wanted to touch base briefly with a few sentences. I am not used to this journal yet at all—beautiful though it is. I love my sweetheart in the front of it—my beloved Rochester. He is so dear, so handsome, my little one. Okay, more soon. I will leave these lovely quotations on the pages as I now leave.

Imagination is Evidence of the Divine.

—William Blake

We have to be braver than we think we can be because God is constantly calling us to be more than we are."

—Madeleine L'Engle

To live in hearts we leave behind, Is not to die.

—Thomas Campbell

The fingerprint of God is often a paw print.

—Susan McElroy

Imagination is the eye of the soul.

—Joseph Joubert

No single telling of a man's story can encompass his life

—in regard to a film about Gandhi, this quote
opens the film, but I do not know
if it is by Gandhi.

A TOUCH OF GRACE

A prayer book of one's own—
like a room of one's own—
is a secret place
a touch of grace—
a hallowed place known
only to God and you alone.

Jan
April 2001

But in my case it is shared with my beloved Rochester—my love and my Angel forevermore!

This poem and the one preceding it by several pages here are both being put in the new book I am writing on prayer.

SUNDAY, JUNE 17, 2001

Happy Father's Day, dear Dad. I just wanted to greet you on paper and tell you that I love you. I have missed you so much. I have written about you a great deal in the book I am writing at present on prayer. I am nearing completion on it. I love you very much and have missed you more than I can say. I have written many poems for you since you left.

EVENING

My writing above is terrible! I wrote it in the morning before Mass and our room is dreary because it was raining and I also did not put my glasses on. But it does not take away the love message for my dad.

The poem I will enter now was written for my book. Though written in April I neglected to enter it in this journal as well as in the manuscript.

NIGHT SYMPHONY

    I lie where
        the moon shines on me.
    The soft wind whispers—
        and each tree
            with its whistling branches
                and green-leaf dances—
                    joins in the symphony
                        of gentle sounds.
    The lake laps
        against the pebbled shore.
    A squirrel runs across the roof—
        and bird call abounds
            into the night.
    And I am alive streaked in moonlight—
        and in the utter mystery
            of it all.

                        Jan
                        April 16, 2001

JUNE 18, 2001

Worked on my book again and on the porch. Too hot still to work up in my room. I am working on the Meditation concerning "Fasting." Chester was with me all the time and Bob comes over from the Birchgrove once in awhile too. He is still typing my book. Have some things I want to enter in here but it is so late I will wait until tomorrow.

The verse that follows is inside a birthday card I sent to Ginny for her May 5th birthday. I just like it. Card had two young girls on it signifying us, of course!

> *You're my spirit-lifting,*
> *joy bringing*
> *gift-giving, love-sending,*
> *heart-mending, problem-solving,*
> *laughter-sharing,*
> *story-telling,*
> *fun-seeking,*
> *forever-friend.*

TUESDAY, JUNE 19, 2001

Just a greeting to my journal in early morning so I can get back into the routine of writing daily. It is another glorious sunny breeze-filled day with our wind chimes dancing and after a few things I have to get out in the mail I will begin writing again on my book. Rochester is already waiting for me out on the screened-in-porch. I think I will write out there again instead of in my room (*our* room, forgive me—Rochester's and mine) because it gets so hot up there in the afternoon.

WEDNESDAY, 1:32 AM, JUNE 20, 2001

I am going to read a little more then sleep. I finished the chapter (meditation) on *fasting* for my book. I am pleased with it. It is quite long. It took me twenty-five minutes to read it just now. I covered many things in it. I also did other writing. Will write about it tomorrow. It is so hot now. Thank you, dear Christ, for helping me to write. Rochester was on the porch with me and Bob came to talk to me at times too. He finished typing the meditation on "The Prayer of Walking."

JUNE 20, 2001

Now it is morning and before I can get back to writing my book and trying to complete it this week, I will garden today for the first time. I wanted to have some flowers in before Janna came this weekend. Bob bought beautiful flowers yesterday down at the flower place in Sanborn-ville— $50.00 worth! This will only get us started, but they are so pretty and I took pictures of them right away. Many kinds!

THURSDAY, JUNE 21, 2001

I was too tired to write in here last night because I read so long. I did plant over half of the flowers Bob bought and they look beautiful. Just put them in three gardens so far, but we will be putting a lot more flowers that I will plant next week. It looks so sweet to see color out there again and the big pots look wonderful filled with a type of two different kinds of a plant the woman called "Profusion"—but it is a type of zinnia. The reddish ones are in the center surrounded by the whites. It felt good to get down on my knees again out there by the rocks and dig in the earth and plant. Today it is very dreary out and cool which we love. We have a lot of cleaning up to do so I cannot work on my book right now. We have really messed our little place up because we have been concentrating on my writing and Bob's typing, the Bookshop, and etc. I am amazed. Bob has a list he made of my chapters for the book I am writing and there are 29! But I have one upstairs to finish, two to write, plus an introduction and perhaps even a closing chapter. Bob will do a "foreword" again at my request. So I have to keep moving to hopefully make my July deadline I have in mind, the anniversary of the day I met Christ.

2:15 PM

I just read that the lotus is not related to the water lily. Lotuses belong with sycamores. I have never heard that in my life. I thought the lotus and waterlily are related.

FRIDAY, JUNE 22, 2001

Good morning—I will write later. Did not finish cleaning up yester-day. Have a lot to do. I cannot wait to get back at my writing so I can get all the writing finished and then spend a lot of time rereading and getting the meditations (chapters) in their right order. Yesterday was cold with rain too, and today is cold and it is supposed to rain. Such a contrast of the heat of last week but we love the coolness.

SATURDAY, JUNE 30, 2001

God is the strength of my heart

—Psalms

I want to use this as a mantra. I just read it in my Angel magazine. They did not give the chapter or verse.

I am on the porch and hopefully I will write the Introduction to my book on Prayer. It would be good too if I decided on a title. I have finished at last the chapter (or "meditation" as I am calling them) on Rochester and Angels, and Poetry. I combined the one on Rochester and Angels. The wind is blowing and it is lovely, but if it stops it is really hot. Supposed to go to the 90s today. Boats are speeding around on the lake. Much noisier on weekends with the boats. My flowers I planted on two afternoons last week are glorious! Just beautiful. And Bob waters them a lot too. We will get more in a few days that I will plant this week, but at the moment I have flowers in every one of my seven gardens.

Patti and children are here for the weekend and have been since Thursday night. Nice! Dennis arriving today. Patti and Michael were with us many hours on the porch here yesterday and it was lovely. We got caught up on a lot of things. We love them like our own family. Laurel and Richard arrived late last night at the Inn with their three boys and Ellen. We will not be seeing them today. They are going out on Michael and Jessica's boat. Talked to Laurel on the phone about 9:20 AM. June and Rob and four children arriving tomorrow. Staying in Rhode Island tonight at George's. Today is Tim's 20th birthday. Will write more later about George.

SUNDAY, JULY 1, 2001

Went to Mass and then to Close to Home for breakfast with Patti and Dennis and kids. We were going to be together when we got home. Bob and Dennis were going to get the boat unpacked and in the lake, but violent storms came up and lasted all afternoon and into early evening. It was terrible and too, frightening! We have not experienced such violent storms even though many were similar. As a result we never saw Dennis and Patti and they called before they left, and we never went to Jessica's church at 7 PM to hear Maxine and Renee sing in a concert or see June, Laurel and crowd. It simply was not wise to go outside in the electrical storms. Dennis and Patti left for home after they were over.

I did get another chapter written for my book, one that suddenly came to mind that I had not intended to write on Hypnogogic Imagery (also known as Twilight Imagery). It is good, I feel, and I am glad it was brought to mind to write because it belongs in this book even though I wrote about it in *Beneath the Stars and Trees* too. I changed it somewhat for this book and added some things as well.

Bob and Chester and I had a nice evening and it was amazing we did not lose our electricity in the heavy storms. There was a lot of news about them on the 11 PM news and lightning hit several homes. It was scary!

TUESDAY, JULY 3, 2001

I wrote the poem for the "Twilight Imagery" chapter in bed last night about 12:30 AM before sleep. It just poured out as many others have done before that time of morning. I had left a page blank for a poem in case one came so I was able to write it in this morning in this journal.

TWILIGHT IMAGERY

What can it mean—
        each miniature scene
                upon the inner eye?
Angel and unicorn
        instantly born
                then fly!
Present and past
        images leave me aghast
                at precise detail.
Gift from above?
        O there's a white dove!
                What next will unveil?

From conception!
Each perfection!

Appear—endear!
Cheer—disappear!

Jan
July 3, 2001

SATURDAY, JULY 21, 2001

Have been so negligent about writing in here. It makes me so upset. but with family having been here and all my writing and proof realizing I just have not written in here. I will try to do better. Rob drove up to New Hampshire from Jenkintown arriving last night and is at the Inn. We went up to be with him this morning and spent one and a half hours. The three of us had a good talk and Jess gave us breakfast. I have been on the porch for a long time working on my book. Chester is here with me. He is so precious. I hate to leave him. It is a beautiful day with lovely breezes. Lots of boats on the lake because it is a weekend. Just being here with Chester is perfection. I love him so much it can not be written. He is stretched out sound asleep near me.

JULY 26, 2001

Why do I frequently need to protect myself from those who say they love me.
—Ashleigh Brilliant

TUESDAY, AUGUST 7, 2001

It is official now. I am going to call my new book on prayer:
Beside the Still Waters: Creative Prayer from the Woods
I love this. I have had it in my mind for a long time. I will discuss it later. The main title, of course, is from the 23rd Psalm.

FRIDAY, AUGUST 10, 2001

Still yet another change. The title of my new book is:
Beside the Still Waters: Creative Meditations from the Woods
I felt "meditations" more appropriate since each chapter is called "Meditation" instead of "Chapter." Then it uses "prayer" often in the titles of each of the "Meditations." I am satisfied now with the beautiful title.

Humiliation is the one event in human life that becomes unforgettable. The loss of human dignity at the hands of another can be forgiven, but it is rarely, if ever, forgotten.

—Jamie Sams

Another realization is that healing humiliation and loss of human dignity must come from inside a person. No other can do it for the wounded one, not a doctor, psychologist, healer, or anyone but the person himself, but with the help of God it can be done. Much prayer, mediation, and writing is the spiritual prescription for recovering. It is true!

The words on the opposite page, all of them, are in my new book *Beside the Still Waters: Creative Meditations from the Woods.*

AUGUST 15, 2001, FEAST OF THE ASSUMPTION

I partly filled a big bottle that had held grape juice with water from our lake. It is on this Feast of Mary's that it is said she blesses all the waters of the earth. I usually try to bottle some for use as our Holy Water. Last year I missed doing this.

I am nearing completion of the checking of my manuscript, the adding, deleting and correcting. Have already totally read it through plus many chapters I have read many times. We will finish tomorrow.

My beloved Rochester is always near me, my Angel. We will be going to Rhode Island Saturday for a party (picnic) George is having for Val's 30th birthday. So nice! But I hate to leave my Chester alone. He will be comfortable as always but will be anxiously awaiting inside the door when we return. I believe he knows and senses we are returning when we are still miles from home.

Tell me what it is you plan to do with your one wild and precious life?

—Unknown

Whatever sustains the soul may turn out to sustain and lengthen life as well.

—Jean Shinoda Bolen, MD

My book is totally completed! Hallelujah! My part is finished. Bob is now about to make a copy of it to send to Paul. It all looks beautiful. I am proud of it and just took three pictures of it.

Bob made a copy of my manuscript to send to Paul. We will keep the one in the loose leaf book. He also put the manuscript on disk that we will send too. I have them all on the kitchen table with an Angel on top of them. I will put them up on my desk on Sunday while our Clancys are here. I will be mailing the manuscript and disk on Tuesday, August 21, the 24th anniversary of my dad's death. My dad will help me. The book is already accepted and published according to the way of prayer affirmations.

MY DAD'S 24TH ANNIVERSARY OF DEATH
AUGUST 21, 2001

If the dead be truly dead, why should they be walking in my heart?
—Winneap Shosone, Medicine man

My dad is always walking in my heart. I have written so much about him in the book I just completed. I miss him with all my heart and love him with all my heart. No one remembers it is his anniversary of death. If they do they do not say it to me ever, year after year. The same with my Mother. Bob knows, of course, because I was aiming for this day to mail in my manuscript, but he would not remember, I feel certain, if I had not mentioned it. He is oblivious to significant dates. I am not criticizing him. Many people are like that. It is just the way he is. And I am the opposite. But Bob never, never forgets our anniversary or my birthday or Valentine's Day or holidays we share together. Never! Dates are very important to me concerning loved ones and animals and people I care about.

Today I mailed my new manuscript *Beside the Still Waters: Creative Meditations from the Woods*. Please, dear Christ, please let me hear soon the words of acceptance. Today I am believing my manuscript will be accepted in three weeks time or less like my *The Enchantment of Writing* was. I claim that and thank Jesus in advance.

I repeat this quotation I entered earlier in this journal to honor my dad.

> *To live in hearts we leave behind, is not to die.*
> —Thomas Campbell

You live in my heart, dear Dad, forever and ever. You have never died.

SEPTEMBER 2, 2001

> *Life is too short to be taking care of the wrong details.*
> —Alexandra Stoddard

6:45 AM

Have just finished five minutes ago a wonderful book—perhaps not for everyone, but certainly for me. I felt the need to record it right away and then just think about it. The book is *Celebrating Time Alone: Stories of Splendid Solitude.* Does that sound like me or what? The author is Lionel Fisher, published in 2001 by Beyond Words Publishing, Inc. in Hillsboro, Oregon. I bought it last week in Barnes and Noble. I will explain that later. I just needed to record the book because I fail to record others that I intend to record.

I had a dream early this morning before waking, actually two. Both were vivid yet when I was awake only minutes, the second dream began to disappear from my memory and I could not capture even a fragment of it. But I have remembered the first dream and I was foolish to wait so long to record it because I lose so many of them.

> *I was in a room with several long windows that had shades and I think blinds too on them. The windows went down fairly close to the floor. Outside on a porch was a huge bear trying to get in. Just the massive head and shoulders could be seen in the dream. I was inside this strange house (I do not know the house) and I was trying to get Chester off the floor and did so I could carry him to escape from the bear. There was a little guinea pig there too, and another woman older with a fancy hat on. I believed her*

to be Eleanor Roosevelt though she nor I ever said who she was. She was carrying the guinea pig on her shoulder as we tried to get out of the room. We first pulled down the shade (the blind too, I think) to cover the window in an attempt to keep out the bear—but we could not get the window down. This is why we were trying to escape. What does it mean?

I dreamed of "windows" in a dream this past year that is recorded in one of my journals or notebooks. I will have to look it up and also pray about this present dream to try and receive an interpretation.

> May I be happy...
> > May I be peaceful...
> > > May I be free from suffering.
>
> May you be happy...
> > May you be peaceful...
> > > May you be free from suffering.

SUNDAY, JANUARY 20, 2002

In all these months I have not been able to write in this journal. It is not totally explainable. I have tried to write in here so many times and I simply could not. I have tried to begin writing a new book and could not. It has only been in the last three weeks I was able to write three or four short things that are to be part of a new book. I had finished writing my book on prayer *Beside the Still Waters* and mailed it into Blue Dolphin on my dad's anniversary of death, August 21, 2001. I had intended to take a short vacation of about four weeks and then begin another book. But September 11th happened and devastated me and I have never been the same. No matter how hard I tried or sat down with paper and pencil I could not begin to write. I cried many times in frustration but I cried much more daily for the events of September 11th and all the things that continue to happen because of the horrendous events of that day. I decided today I would not leave my writing room until I wrote something in this journal and I have been here a long time until I finally opened this journal, got a new pen from the box and began to write. I cannot let this happen again. I have to force myself. These months since September 11th have been so difficult and I have felt empty, and too at a loss, because

I lost the ability to write, the very thing that would have helped me as we have learned of the daily events connected to September 11th. I will stop now with a promise to write more tomorrow, and the next day and the next.

I must write. So many things to write about.

MONDAY, JANUARY 21, 2002

Each friend represents a world in us,
a world possibly not born until they arrive,
and it is only by this meeting that a new world is born.

—Anais Nin

Today is Martin Luther King Day and I believe New Hampshire was the last state to adopt it as a holiday just two years ago. I had not realized he was shot dead in April, I believe April 14, 1968, and therefore I will have to learn why we remember him specifically today. I would assume it is his birthday. It must be and I am very stupid to have even written this or wondered why. I was moved by what I saw on CNN and other ones and it made me so sad so I guess my brain is not working. I remember when the assassination happened, of course, and all these years later it is still so extremely horrendous and terrible. I relive the events of September 11th every day and go over and over it in my heart and mind. Janna was not yet born when the assassination occurred. It seems impossible. I am so sorry his family has been without him all these years. I am so stupid! Of course today is his birthday! It was announced he was 73 today.

We are having another snow storm and it is beautiful outside. We had snow Saturday night and into yesterday morning too.

LATER

I have just finished writing another meditation or whatever I am going to call them—for my new book yet untitled. I like what I have written. It was a chapter on a specific kind of prayer and it helped me to write about it because I then used that form of prayer for myself in regard to a deep concern I have. I received a comforting answer and will perhaps enter it in there tomorrow. We will see. I have to do things to help myself.

TUESDAY, JANUARY 22, 2002

Edward Mazzella WTC

Today in the mail I received the bracelet I ordered bearing the name of a person who died in the World Trade Center disaster of September 11th. His name is above. It meant so much to receive it.

Postscript (June 6, 2008): I have worn this sterling silver cuff bracelet for Edward since I received it and have never removed it and never shall. Like Rochester's collar that I also wear, both will remain together forever on my left arm.

MONDAY, JANUARY 28, 2002

Barb is coming here to be with us. it is wonderful! I will write in more detail soon. An unusual thing happened regarding her phone call tonight.

JANUARY 29, 2002

So busy today getting ready for Barb. I am so happy. We will meet her in Newington at 4:15 PM tomorrow.

WEDNESDAY, JANUARY 30, 2002

Ta-dah! Barbie is here. Picked her up at 4:15 PM. As always the bus came in exactly on time—just like each bus always leaves exactly on time too. It was so good to see Barb. She looks great and I love her pretty long curly hair. How I wish my hair was like that. We went to dinner at Bickfords in Newington mall and that was enjoyable. We told her she could go to any of the stores if she wanted to, but she chose to come directly home. By this time she was not feeling well.

Though I have made many entries about our daughter Barbara while she was visiting, I have chosen to not include most so as to keep her privacy.

THURSDAY, JANUARY 31, 2002

Life is not life at all without delight.
—Coventry Patmore (1823–1896)

A dream is an unopened letter to yourself.
—The Talmud

For when you journey inward, you will never be without.
—Susan Castle

Author Burghild Nina Holzer says:

Most people have no idea that writing takes time. I do not mean just the time that you sit at the desk, but the time it takes for dreaming the new child into manifestation. The creative process is a gestation process, and it cannot be pushed.

How well I know this and have experienced it many times often to the point of tears, feeling like I am empty inside and will never be able to write again.

She says you cannot push this process and it is exactly correct to do as I do. That you need to sit around and do nothing. Yes, and stare into space as I do too, and dream and play. I know it to be true because it has happened to me and again that then all the while some mysterious process is going on inside you long before you are ready to write. This is the kind of time I need alone with Rochester up in our writing room. I need to shift realities and enter a new dimension. To anyone else it might look like I am wasting the day—but no no. I need many many times like this and then suddenly I slip into that other reality and begin to write and write. Amen! (I believe my family thinks I always live in that other reality. Perhaps I do.)

I understand all of this so well and experience it. It is frustrating at times. It was like this last time after I finished *Beside the Still Waters* and could not begin another book. It was so upsetting. This, combined with September 11th, left me different and upset and wiped out and teary, and I could barely begin a new book. And I need to write! It helps me in all aspects of my life.

5:45 PM

I have been reading and writing down things in relation to what I want to write tomorrow and insights into things I want to include in this book I am working on. The snow continues to fall heavily. Rochester is asleep on the sofa beside me because we cannot be up in our writing room because we have given it over to Barb and we are so thankful she is here. Rochester visits her up there occasionally.

I am reading (I go back to it so often) *A Walk Between Heaven and Earth: A Personal Journal to Writing and the Creative Process* by Burghild Nina Holzer. I have mentioned this author and her book in my books. it is a wonderful book from her heart on journaling and always inspired me when I need motivation when I am having trouble beginning a new book. But I love picking it up anytime. Wish I could talk to her. I recorded something from her book two pages or so previous to this.

10:30 PM

We four are all here together talking and watching TV; Bob, Barb,, Chester and myself. A lovely time. I made mashed potatoes, corn, apple-sauce and chick pats (Barb) and Prime Burgers (Bob and me) for dinner. Barb does not mind eating our vegetarian "meat' products when here—in fact she really enjoys them. Chester had something he liked too.

FRIDAY, FEBRUARY 1, 2002

Some snow when we woke. Eventually Johnny Blackwood came, promptly for Johnny, and ploughed our hill. Bob made us Cream of Wheat for breakfast and I made toast and veggie bacon and it was all delicious and we had fun talking. It is so good to have Barbie here.

1:52 AM

Had a wonderful evening together, or I should say an entire day. Barb slept for several hours in the afternoon and when she did I worked on a chapter or meditation in the new book I am writing. It was on the subject of dreams. After I made dinner and we enjoyed it together the three of us played Scrabble together and we played at the kitchen table for an hour and a half and had so much fun. It was very special and we are going to do it again. We watched TV then and *Nightline* wiped me out. It was Ted Koppel covering Ground Zero and talking to retired firemen who lost family members and who came there to Ground Zero everyday to work and try to find bodies and belongings. I am overwhelmed by it all. It was part of my writing today too in that chapter I am working on. I will write more about the program later.

Chester is so precious and so dear with us all day. As I have written he cannot go up in our writing room to sleep because of Barb, so he hangs out and then naps on the sofa so close and pressed up to me while I write. I love him so much. He is eating so much more. Doing so great! I pray about it always—every day. The Blessed Mother is helping me.

SATURDAY, FEBRUARY 2, 2002

Woke up to find the electricity was off. Bob called about it but it was not going to be off long. They said it would return by 10 AM but it was on much earlier. Shades of the ice storm of several years ago each time we lose electricity. Bob, Barb and I are going to have breakfast and then play Scrabble before Barb goes up to the Inn for the weekend with Jessica. I will stop now and make the eggs.

Postscript: Barb will be going to The Hitching Post Village Inn in Center Ossipee, New Hampshire, 25 minutes north of us that is owned and run by Michael and Jessica since 1994.

TUESDAY, FEBRUARY 5, 2002

Got behind in my entries but that is okay. I am now back in sync I feel, because I am reminding myself to write in here and looking forward to it. We took Barb to the Inn mid-afternoon Saturday and we stayed just a short while. Jessica's friend Deanna was there for the weekend with daughter Stacy and their beautiful and unusual bird. Her name was "Tequilla" after "Tequilla Sunset" because she was all white and gorgeous and under her feathers were shades of coral and pink and a bit near her eyes too. She talked and was affectionate and was in a tall white cage. She looked so pretty in it. At one point Deanna took her out of her cage wrapped in a sweater. She was so sweet. She got loose and was flying all over the kitchen and sitting on our heads. Finally Deanna put her back.

All the time I talked to her while she was in the cage she would bend her little head down against the bars so I would scratch it—and I did! I talked to her and petted her chest and she would say things to me I could not quite understand. Such a sweet little bird. I was so glad I met her. We eventually left and it was good to get back to our cozy cottage and my beloved little Chester. We three had dinner and a perfect evening together and we were where we wanted to be.

Sunday Bob and I went to Mass and then to breakfast at Close to Home. Nice!! The rest of the day Bob was watching basketball games on TV. It was a great day and I wrote for hours and read and Chester was ever with me. It was an unusual day totally filled with sports from the time we came home from church until we went to sleep almost. I am so thankful Barbie is here and I will meet her and Jessica early morning in Wolfeboro in "Made on Earth," our favorite store.

Before speaking, consider whether it is an improvement upon silence.
—an Indian Yogi

FEBRUARY 4, 2002

Yesterday morning we got back together again and spent an hour or more in "Made On Earth" while Bob did a few errands. I bought a book I am anxious to begin titled *Learning to Fall: The Blessings of an Imperfect Life* by Philip Simmons. He is a New Hampshire author. I will write more about it after I begin to read it. The girls got some jewelry (they have unique things there) and I treated them each to something too. They were kidding me because I stay in the book section all the time until they force me out. I am thankful to have found this book by Philip Simmons. I know I am supposed to read it. The girls have no interest in the book section here because the store has so many interesting imports and clothes as well as the jewelry. I did manage to show them three of my books on the shelves though: *Compassion For all Creatures*, *Journal of Love* and *The Enchantment of Writing*. What a moving time for me all alone as I discovered the latter two on the shelves. They have carried *Compassion* for some time but not the others. I got all teary by myself. It means so much. Eventually I called the girls over to see all three of my books on the shelves but it made little impact because they were interested in other things not having been here in a long while. But they did say, "That's nice, Mom" and were just being themselves as they kidded around and then went back to jewelry. Because it was so amazing to discover my books (I mean how often do you see three books you have written on shelves together in a store?) I wanted to share it all with them even though books were surely not their main interest. I normally go to that store alone. It was unusual they were with me when I discovered my books. It gave me such joy and I felt honored to have them in this particular store that is so unique and is my favorite and the owner Marybeth is so lovely. Bob was pleased to hear about it afterwards. And I felt so blessed to be with both Jessica and Barb in New Hampshire! So unusual! I love them so much.

We picked up the Veggie Bacon we ordered at the Health Food Store and then took the girls out for lunch at Louis Pizza in Wolfeboro and we had fun together. Jessica left us then to go back to the Inn and Bob, Barb and I came on home to little Chester who was waiting.

It gives me such joy Barb is here.

Again I will not include the next several pages of this journal for they belong to Barb and her privacy.

THURSDAY, FEBRUARY 7, 2002

Today we took Barbie to the bus in Newington where we had picked her up a week and a half ago. Her bus left at 10 AM and we went to Bickford's to have breakfast first just as we had eaten dinner there when she arrived Wednesday afternoon over a week ago (January 31). We all had a delicious breakfast. How I hated to see her board the bus. We took one picture of her before she boarded and she and I kept throwing kisses and waving as she sat inside the bus. It was hard to see her because of the tinted windows. She wore the pink scarf I made for her. So cute of her to do that but she seemed to like it so much. I forgot to enter that after we left Barb at Jessica's mid-afternoon last Saturday I began knitting a pink scarf for Barb. I worked on it Saturday night and all Sunday afternoon after church and finished it. It is so pretty. Baby pink. She loves pink. It was seven feet or so long and narrow and she could wrap it around her neck loosely or more than once. She looked pretty in it. I was shocked I finished knitting it in such a short time but I wanted to do it when she was at Jess's.

I am so sad Barbie is gone but she called us to say she arrived home safely and it was so good to hear her voice.

After we left Barbie off at the bus we went to Barnes and Noble (or I did) and Bob did a few errands. I will write of it another time. It was like therapy in many ways and especially after parting with Barb. I was lost in the books and I will write a specific entry about my time in there because it was so special and healing. We had a nice evening and it was so good to be with Chester. We had arrived at our Post Office right before it closed (at 3:15 PM) and then came home. Chester and I spent the rest of the day and night together as always.

I love this!!! (It is speaking of New Hampshire.)

If our town were a country its national flag would be a blue tarp.
    —Philip Simmons (a New Hampshire writer), *Learning to Fall*

FRIDAY, FEBRUARY 8, 2002

An unusual thing happened again tonight right after I ended writing and Bob closed up shop at the Birchgrove.

I was meditating after writing on my new book before going downstairs. This happened about 6:40 PM. I was in deep meditation and I cannot say if I was in "that state" when this happened or if I had momentarily entered sleep. Rochester was with me.

I saw Bob (in this prayer reverie) coming indoors to our cottage. I heard his office door slam, then silence. Then I heard the porch door shut loudly, then I heard our inner door open and heard Bob call up—"Jan." It brought me out of the deep reverie or meditation and I was startled. But I did nothing and decided to wait silently in my chair.

Seconds later as I sat in my chair I heard Bob's office door slam, then silence as I knew he was walking over. Then I heard the porch door shut loudly. Then I heard our inner door open and Bob called "Jan." This made me smile.

The reverie I experienced in vivid detail and that woke me or brought me out of meditation with Bob calling "Jan" was repeated exactly in detail in real life. It was incredible! Who can explain such things? There are other dimensions and realms! This was so amazing, like an exact rerun in real life of an other dimension!!!!

Bob and I and Chester watched the opening of the Winter Olympics tonight. It was on for many hours and was a real extravaganza and very special. Am back to my writing of my next book that I only did very limited things on while Barb was here— really just more like jotting down thoughts. I look forward to working on it now.

TUESDAY, FEBRUARY 12, 2002

Two things big in the news this morning! They captured the man who headed up the kidnapping of Daniel Pearl, the reporter kidnapped three weeks ago that I have been praying for every day. He was kidnapped either in Pakistan or Afghanistan when he went there to investigate the "shoebomber" that was arrested on a plane some weeks ago. They say this man they arrested knows where Daniel Pearl is in Pakistan and that he is alive and could be released as early as today. Please God, let him be still alive and be released. He is only 38 years old. His wife is six months pregnant here in the United States. I have been praying every day as have countless others I am certain. Please help him, dear God.

The other news is that reports have come in from many sources that another bombing is planned somewhere in the United States and that too, could come as early as today. It is frightening! Some have speculated it could be at the Winter Olympics and all precautions are being taken, but how can they protect from a bombing such as happened September 11th in all these places?

I did not write anything about the weekend or yesterday but I will. Talked to Barbie yesterday so I want to write about that. And talked to Jess today and so many strange things go on in our family. I want to get back to my writing now. Rochester is here with me as always.

Before I sleep I want to add that yesterday February 11th was Uncle Elmer's birthday. Had I had time to write I would have headed up the page with that announcement. I wrote another meditation for my new book yesterday, "In God We Trust" (title of the meditation not the book). I love Uncle Elmer very much and will always love him and I pray for him and ask him to help me in many ways especially with my writing. I think he would be 101 years old. He was always so sweet and good to me and to Bob and all our children. He is a part of my life always. I do not need his birthday to mention him but I just wanted to do so. I have written about him especially in my *Enchantment of Writing*. I love you, Uncle Elmer.

5:40 PM

Have just finished writing my meditation on "Dreams." I had begun it before Barb arrived and added much more to it today. Barb is very much in it though not by name. I like it. I have reread twice. I am beginning now the meditation about my Mercy Band and the significance of wearing one.

THURSDAY, FEBRUARY 14, 2002

Yesterday I wrote my meditation about my Mercy B.A.N.D. and I think I covered every aspect of it. It was so good to be working upstairs with Rochester with me. This is a little poem I wrote to include in the meditation—but I wrote it in bed this morning.

MERCY B.A.N.D.

A simple band
Worn daily with pride—
Bearing the name
Of one who died.

Jan

Remembering Edward Mazzella now and always
Died September 11, 2001—World Trade Center

*Every day is a renewal,
every morning the daily miracle.
This joy you feel is life.*

—Gertrude Stein

SING

Be like the grackle!
Earnestly tackle—
Any timidity of voice.
Make now the choice—
To sing out your song.
It will never be wrong—
For it comes from your heart
Where all love notes start.

Jan
February 14, 2002
—for one of my meditations just written for my new book.

REVERIE

A scene from the past
Appears in reverie
I am taking repast
On boardwalk by the sea.
In restaurant of old
I sit as before—
And watch episode unfold
As enchanting timeless lore.

Such mysteries are vast
That memories arrive
And moments from the past
Become surrealistically alive.

Jan
February 11, 2002

Three new poems after not having written any since I completed my last book and sent it in August 21, 2001

All came after I was in bed after 1:30 AM. One came shortly after I woke, the other two before I slept. Each is for one of my new meditations in the book I am working on.

Wrote another meditation today for the book I am working on about the feeding of the workers at Ground Zero by a restaurant. The owners fed everyone free—no charge, since September 11th. They just closed their restaurant about a week ago.

LATER ON SATURDAY, FEBRUARY 9. 2002

On Saturday, February 9th, Princess Margaret of England died at only age 71. I may have entered this before. I felt so sad for her. Her own mother is still alive at 101 years.

She is being buried today on the 50th anniversary of the burial of her father King George VI. She is being cremated at her own request in order to be laid to rest with him, cremated today.

The Queen Mother at 101 years was helicoptered in for the services. It took forty minutes. She lives three and a half hours away and she could not stand a trip of that length by car.

This year Queen Elizabeth will be celebrating 50 years on the throne of England and it is such a shame her sister will not be with her. I think the Queen is 76 years. Princess Margaret died of a stroke. It is all on CNN and most interesting. It has been mentioned all week but a lot more was shown this morning. Princess Margaret had had other strokes. She lived a faster life of smoking and drinking it was reported and as a result her health was affected. I feel so sad. I am sure she has suffered a lot emotionally though in the shadow of her sister.

THIS CONCLUDES THIS JOURNAL.

Rochester

On his shelf on the porch
January 2002
entered Heaven
March 8, 2002

MEDITATION TEN

Friday Miracles—
Gifts from Mary
and Rochester

*... counting beads has been used as a tool in praying for centuries, and
has been adopted in many different cultures and religions.
For me, the Rosary is just that—a tool, a focal point, and a telephone
of sorts—which helps me start what I refer to as
a "Prayer Dialogue" with God.*

—John Edward

DURING THE WRITING OF THIS BOOK I have lost two items of jewelry
that are so important to me because one belongs to my dad and
the other was written about elsewhere in this journal recorded of some
years ago at the time it entered my life. I realize we are not to be concerned with the little material objects in our possession but when you
love loved ones it is hard to lose a belonging of someone you love who
is now in Heaven.

Therefore when I recently lost still yet another item in addition
to the two written about, I was really discouraged. This was a pewter
medal bearing the image of Mother Mary under the title of Our Lady
of Guadalupe. This had a significance to Rochester and myself and I
began wearing it shortly after he passed. I never remove the silver chain
that contains this medal along with a small silver star with a star cutout
in its center through which the chain passes. I have always referred to

Rochester as "my star" and it is a symbol for him. I have no idea how
the medal could have been lost from the chain. The silver loop it is on
was tight and secure.

On a recent Friday in August after having my Holy Hour for Rochester on the screened in porch, and somewhere in that Hour asking that
I recover the medal—I stood to go indoors. There lying at my feet was
a plain oval object. I picked it up only to discover it was our medal of
Mary. I was astounded and excited for I had just prayed again to find it!
The silver loop that was through the medal was tight and secure. There
was no way it could have gotten from my chain that I never remove.
Bob too was amazed at it all and to try to cheer me concerning this
third loss he previously had printed out a lovely sheet from on-line with
the familiar story of "Our Lady of Guadalupe" and a beautiful picture
of her image. This was all in her bright colors as was the border. I had
asked her help and Rochester's to find this medal and it came back to
me, actually laid at my feet, while I sat praying
her Rosary and on Rochester's Holy day of
Friday! It made me cry in all its meaning and
its recovery. It was a gift from them both
to affirm anew that they are always with
me for I had been downcast over some
serious matters in my life and very much
so about losing this spiritual medal. I
believe they were telling me anew "we
are ever here." Bob was there when I
ended my prayers and found the medal
at my feet so he too knows my wonder
at this miracle and my appreciation.
He too had amazement at this miracle.
I had used this same chair many times
since I lost the medal for I often proofread this manuscript on the porch and
this medal had not ever been there. I
share with you now a picture of Our
Lady of Guadalupe dressed in colorful
robes. Her gown is red trimmed in white
cuffs and neckline—and her hooded cape
is a soft green. She is beautiful and I wish

you could see her in these lovely colors. A halo of gold is all around her. Her statue identical to this stands in our writing/prayer room next to Rochester's picture.

This poem I have shared at previous times expresses anew all I felt as I sat praying in the prevailing breezes from our lake.

THE PRAYER-FILLED BREEZE

If I could do just as I please—
I'd pray my Rosary in the breeze.
Submit to nature's soft control
To lift and heal my sagging soul.

The beads would through my fingers slip—
While wind would o'er me gently strip—
Those burdens that once held a grip
Send them sailing like a ship!

A precious peace would fill the space
Where once deep wounds held upper place.
And as the wooden beads I'd pray—
Again I'd trod His Blessed Way.

Mother Mary takes me there
The breeze accompanies me in prayer.
The wind and Rosary I acclaim
Hail Mary! Call upon her name!

Written in   Jan
the prayer chair   August 18, 1990
in the breeze

If all of that was not blessing enough, the next Friday I again had my Holy Hour in the same Adirondack chair on the screened in porch. Upon completing it and before standing, I looked down at my Rosary and Rochester's flowered tin containing his precious ashes that I always hold during that hour. There on the front of my white blouse in the soft fold was something silver, only partially seen. I took it from the fold and it was a small silver cross just under an inch or so. It was just the outline of a cross with an empty center.

I have never in my life seen this cross before. My eyes are always closed during that hour as I pray and go into a deep place of peace. Only heavenly intercession of a sort I cannot explain could have placed that cross in the fold of my blouse. I believe it was Mary or Rochester but more likely Rochester. He has left me gifts from the afterlife at other times that have brought me to tears. *Yes, he is ever here!* I keep my new silver cross in my Rosary purse with the Rosary I was praying that day.

Still yet another lovely miracle occurred on a Holy Day of Mary's, August 15th. It again was also a Friday, Rochester's Holy Day. After a very long period of my last and newest book *Silent Keepers* lying dormant for many months after acceptance and without progress—I had a lovely e-mail from my publisher. He wrote of it being Mary's Day and this had been significant to us both for it is the day she is said to bless all the waters of the world. I had often sent him and others there small containers of our lake water on her day of blessing. Now he was saying that progress would begin on my book and it was a loving e-mail of hope. It was a blessed miracle on Mary's Day and Rochester's and again on a Friday!

I cannot close this meditation without leaving some beautiful flowers with you in spirit. Try to imagine them in your heart. If you own a copy of my recent book *Cherishing*—a picture is on the cover of this colorful bloom of which I received two.

My first memory plant for Rochester that I have written about elsewhere in this Journal has not bloomed in two years though it is on a low table and its branches almost touch the ceiling. It is inside the sliding glass doors receiving much light.

On July 25th, a Friday once again (and also our daughter Barbara's birthday) we woke to discover a glorious bud on the Hibiscus. It really was a gift and miracle on Rochester's Day! By evening it was fully open and I took pictures and sat next to it and under it all evening with Rochester's spirit on my legs. The next morning it began to close and by midday was tight. By evening it had dropped and I carefully saved it. Hibiscus blooms are glorious but have a short life.

What can I say but tell you that the very next Friday August 1st I woke again to another bud! The exact same procedure took place and I had it once again until midday Saturday. These flowers meant so much in their significance and holiness to me. They are signs from Rochester in the midst of a time when I was weakened within and feeling sad and not understanding these troubling circumstances.

I had even awakened one morning with a poem inside of me. I had gone to sleep praying about things that are very hurtful to me and when I woke the poem was there and I could barely write it down fast enough in my steno pad that was right by my bed. (Now it is recorded in my journal and here on this page)

Hurts

I feel sad
Depleted, twisted—
Bent and wounded
All tight fisted.
Tears flow out
And I know why—
Too many times
I sit and cry.

August 6, 2008   Jan

It was so amazing and beautiful to receive this poem even though I have received precious writings and instructions and poems before in this manner.

Light and love and actual physical gifts came to me from Rochester and Mother Mary all in a period of several weeks and all on the Holy Day to us of Friday. These were not coincidences. These were God-incidences. I do not believe in coincidences. These were from loved ones in Heaven with God and I am ever grateful and astounded.

Would you be surprised if I told you these blessings are all written of in my journal just as they are written of in this book? I think you would not be surprised. You knew.

I share a poem now in closing that has great tenderness and deep meaning to me that I have placed in one or two of my previous books because the story it tells matters so to me. It always shall. The love and remembrance of each detail is a part of me forever.

SETTLING IN

Little furry face and head—
An inch from mine—I lie in bed.
He stares into my eyes and purrs
Then walks my body—he prefers—
To settle down on legs awhile,
Then moves to tummy—he knows I'll—

Not move an inch—he's here to stay
Because he knows now that we'll pray,
I with my Rosary—now the beads—
Know too, sweet paws and purrs and kneads.
In union with the breaths I take—
He's lulled to sleep until we wake.

Dedicated to Rochester—   Jan
companion in prayer
and all things of life.

Early this morning, the day after writing this meditation, I had a life-like dream of Rochester sitting on the end of the long low coffee table on our screened-in-porch. He sat where the breezes blow in and was staring at me with great love. I woke and knew it was a "visit"—not a dream. Again it was a Holy Blessing on a Friday and he was sitting on the very table that is opposite my Adirondack Chair where I had received my previous blessings and prayed our Rosary.

I am so grateful. His visit is already recorded in my Journal! Are your blessings recorded in yours? Please say "yes."

MEDITATION ELEVEN

Dreams

*Has your precious cat (or dog or any beloved animal) ever entered
your dreams? In your dream state did you learn anything
you had not had understanding of before?*

*Behold, I send an Angel before thee, to keep thee in the way,
and to bring thee into the place which I have prepared.*
—Exodus 23:20

*I*N A LOVELY HARDBACK JOURNAL I have entered only dreams and they
are only dreams in which Rochester appears. The cover depicts a
black and white checkered floor and glass doors that are partially open.
A small white cat has walked out through the doors and is looking at
a glorious full moon shining on a beautiful lush green forest. A green
wooded path lies ahead of the little cat if he should step away from the
black and white floor. It is a very magical cover that attracted me to it
years ago in the Walden Book Store in Rochester, New Hampshire. The
painting on the cover is titled *Blue Moon* and how often I too go out my
door to see the moon shining over our woods—and the path of light it
creates over the lake.

The moon and stars long ago became so deeply spiritual to me and
most especially after moving to these woods. The night sky here I have
written about numerous times in prose and poetry for it is like no other
night sky we have ever observed. It is wondrous with stars so amazing
spread endlessly! It was to the night sky I turned to upon arriving home
with empty arms after Rochester had just gone to Heaven. I stood with
head back and in tears for consolation from the Heavens. I had always

called Rochester "My Star" and "My Angel," his most prominent love names. But the moon also is so meaningful to us. Years ago I wrote a poem when Rochester was with me about this magic of the moon that I will include now. It has even more meaning since 2002 for I know Rochester too is safely in God's Heaven as well as in Spirit with me every moment.

BY THE LAKE

O beautiful moon
Shining on me
Streaming your light
From eternity

Creating a pathway
Straight from the sky
Out onto the water
Beckoning me nigh

Did you wish me to tred
Ever lightly your beam
Or am I imagining
As if in a dream?

Oh, now I see clearly
Why you gloriously glow
God's in His heaven
And you're telling me so.

Jan

Blue Moon, you knew just what I was there for.
You heard me sayin' a prayer for
Someone....

In this journal I speak of, the unusual and precious dreams of Rochester were only in 1997 and 1998. Many other dreams in addition were recorded in my own journals before and after his passing. During the horrendous ice storm of 1998 here in New Hampshire and Maine that left us without power for over a week and in frigid weather (I have written of it in a previous book), I had numerous dreams that revealed the underlying fear and concern I had for the three of us and especially in keeping Rochester warm enough. He could not pile on sweatshirts as we had done. So these dreams centered on him and were most unusual. I am pleased I have them all recorded as well as other dreams of past times in which either he appeared or both of us together. Too, Bob was in several. As I reread them in the present, they show me insights and signs I did not see when first recording them and most all have been comforting. That is why it is important to capture your dreams when possible and write them in your journal. Some advocate a separate journal. Others believe it is best to record dreams in your regular journal for then it is easier to see how they may tie in with your previous entries or daily living and experiences.

As I end these brief thoughts I encourage you to honor your dreams. Though I am not willing to share my dreams from this journal, I will mention in part the last one I recorded. I find it both interesting and utter truth and it makes me cry, for it speaks of how Rochester goes everywhere I go and is everywhere I am. In the dream I carried him *everywhere* and wherever I was he remained lovingly next to me. It is a prophesy within a dream, for though he was always with me here in this cottage day and night throughout the years, since he has passed and is in Spirit he is always with me still. I do carry him in my soul, his Anima, but his presence I sense always and experience tangibly often.

EVERYWHERE

He is near
My little dear—
He is far
He is my Star.

He is without
He is within—
In the silence
In the din.

He sustains
He ordains—
Removes fear
He is here.

For eternal Rochester   Jan

    I experience his presence nightly as well upon my legs where he once slept in body and continues to in Spirit through his signs to me in intense heat and electric vibrational-like currents. He leaves signs about the cottage and other places I go. I have written in detail of these previously in my books since he passed. He speaks to me inside my mind and soul and is a precious eternal gift to me. I write his words in my journals. I remember the nights he would touch my face gently with his soft white marshmallow paw and look into my eyes. They were transcendent moments for us both. I still know the touch of his small soft paw. He is the mirror of our soul.

ALWAYS THERE

Upon my legs
    you sleep each night—
And though your body's
    out of sight—
You impart warmth
    and heat intense—
Our one heart burns—
    with love immense.

Within our heart
    I kneel and bow—
For your eternal
    presence and vow —
And lie awake
    in awe and prayer—
Thanking God
    you slumber there.

For beloved   Jan
Rochester   May 2002

It is written:
    Tell me whom you love, and I'll tell you who you are.
          —African American Folk Saying

SEPTEMBER 11, 2009

Sometime after I made the brief journal entry of January 28, 2002 in my journal of Woodland Colors on page 194 of this book, I came across a journal entry in another journal, a journal not included in this book. It was made shortly after the January 29 entry in 2002. It is something I barely remembered until I reread it in the present of September 2009 while proofreading this book. It meant so much to me upon discovering it, and so I would like to include it now as I close these reflections on dreams.

Yesterday in my writing, I was working on something that occurred in the recent past that Barb (my daughter) was a part of in an unusual way, though she is not named. As mysteriously predicted, the thing happened and she became a part of both the prediction and the event. It involved dreams so it was surreal. The prediction was in a dream, the event in true life. I stopped writing, went downstairs, the phone rang, and it was Barb calling to say she was arriving Wednesday in Portsmouth, New Hampshire from Pennsylvania at the Trailways Bus Center where we often pick her up. All that I had dreamed with Barb in it was relived from her phone call on to her arrival. It was incredible! I share this to say, be careful what you write! This has occurred before at times but not so immediately, and in such trueness to what I had written! It is as if I wrote her into existence (by phone and in actuality)! I am so excited she is coming (for a week!)!!

—2002

Afterword

If you make the effort, beings seen and unseen will help.
There are Angels cheering for us when we lift up our pens,
because they know we want to do it.
—Natalie Goldberg, *Wild Mind*

THERE ARE SO MANY THINGS can be said and written about journal keeping. I have written on this subject in all of my books with different thoughts, suggestions and sharings in each. No matter what the subject matter of each of the books there is a reference and writing within on keeping a journal, for to me, a journal is part of all I do in life. Once you consider journal keeping if you have never done so before, try to motivate yourself in this newly found attempt to act upon it and obtain a journal. You could just grab an old notebook in the house for convenience sake, but I would suggest not. I would proclaim you give it the importance it deserves and treat yourself to a visit to the nearest bookstore and to a journal that attracts you and calls to you. The selection in a book store is enormous (and so exciting to me) and if you pray first and inwardly get a bit excited about this new venture, you will enjoy it. After all, you are going to have this journal as a companion for some time so you want the cover design, the color, the size and the type paper, and whether it is lined or unlined, to all draw you to it daily or as often as possible. It is a unique experience to pick out a journal.

Later you may receive a journal occasionally as a gift and that is lovely too, but if it is not meant for you when you receive it at that particular time (you will know) just wait and save it, for often in the future it is the perfect one then you want to write in. I have had that happen many times. Do not begin to write in one you do not like. And I enjoy giving journals as gifts, but with full perception that it may not be the very journal that person needs at that moment in time but they will have it as a love gift if they ever do. Too, it may be used as a motivator and a reminder plus it also gives the message that a journal is important. A person may wish a certain type journal in regard to its use. If it is to be a journal for all reasons and seasons then there is such an amazing variety on the shelves! But if it is to be a companion to help you through grief, then one may be even more particular. You will want to write about the memories of the life you shared with your human or animal companion. A journal is extremely helpful at particularly sad times, when grief is overwhelming and your emotions are devastated. It is most important all during the travelling of this journey.

You may pick a cover that relates to your loved one and to your relationship. Art stores also carry wonderful journals and large and small bound sketch books that can be used as journals. It is much finer to have a bound book than to jot your thoughts and memories on loose paper. You will have your book forever filled with the sad and joyful—all of which were and are a part of you and your relationship with your beloved animal or human, (and with yourself). You may use several journals, filling one after another if you are particularly inclined to write. This is good! Your loved one will always be a part of you and be written about in years to come, no matter how many journals you go on to use. You can also write poems in your journal (I do!), or if you cannot, you may see poems or quotations written by others in books or magazines that apply to your dear one and you can copy them in, to be scattered amongst your own writings and feelings. To keep a journal is healing, and it is a private place to meet your precious animal or human in thoughts and prayers (you may compose written prayers for him or her) and through your personal writing that will pour out from your soul. I know this will help you.

I have actually filled identical journals repeatedly in the past until the need to use a journal with a specific cover lessened. I have been in the process of this also in regard to Rochester. Though it may not seem important to another, colors and patterns can be healing and calming and draw the grieving ones to write This applies to persons not grieving also. In my *Solace of Solitude* I confide:

Journal writing is enforced reflection. When we commit our heart and observations to the page, we are taking what is inside of us and boldly placing it outside us. And when we hold our journal in our hands to look at what we have written we are holding a piece of our life in our hands.

Sometimes because I began a journal that I was really not fond of but thought it would not matter, I had to stop in the middle and actually make apologies to the journal, (I am very strange) but I simply had no desire to write in it. Of course these few journals are saved along with all my completed ones, but when I began then a journal that spoke to my heart I wrote up a storm and completed it each time.

When Rochester passed I was consumed with grief and did not leave our woods until Monday March 18th. He had gone to Heaven on Friday, March 8th. I wrote elsewhere in a previous journal:

We decide to go that Monday and our destination is the Walden Book Store in Rochester, twenty-five miles away. It is the town in which I adopted my beloved little Rochester, thus his name. It was also to this town and store I first came before making a week long retreat alone with Rochester three months after he came into my life. We had come from Pennsylvania for this retreat.

Ever since Rochester came to us I would say prayers of gratitude for him in our lives whenever we drove through or past the town of Rochester or anywhere near the spot where we adopted him. I always will do this.

I did not read books on grieving back when I wrote *Beneath the Stars and Trees* in late 1999 and Spring and Summer of 2000. I was grieving for another reason. It was terrible. I had Rochester's physical presence always then however, so comforting. Writing was my total therapy—and prayer, for writing is prayer to me too. And the continual presence of Rochester! But nothing can compare to the loss of Rochester's physical presence. NOTHING! I do need books to read about grieving in regard to Chester as I relate in my *Corridors of Eternal Time* and I buy four. I also buy a beautiful journal to use just to write in about Chester; his life, his passing, and my continued new life with him in *presence*. I will put his messages to me in it just as I kept a journal with all his messages in before he passed away. Many of these are in his book and mine, *Journal of Love*, about communicating with animals through writing that I have written about elsewhere in this book.

> *The new journal I find is so perfect. The night sky here in New Hampshire is always so brilliant with stars and the moon in all its forms, and it is a magic and spiritual part of living here. It was part of my life with Chester. I wrote poems for him comparing him to the stars and angels. He is both of these in my life forever—and ever. This new journal has two half moons facing each other and touching at their points forming a whole, which speaks of an eternal circle to me and Rochester's and my forever and unbroken eternal love. The journal is even titled "Forever" above the moon, which confirms it is meant for my Rochester and my entries about him, and our life together. Stars twinkle on a darkened sky behind the moon, and the sky is deep shades of night blue and red. The cover is light tan, and the trim on the journal is red, a symbol of the one heart we share. It has a red elastic strap to slip over the cover to keep it closed. It is the perfect journal for sacred notes, poems and his life. He is in all of my own personal journals and written about again and again—but this is his journal for past, present, and future—and I will get another just like it if I soon fill the pages as I do with my own journals.*

And I did fill the pages of that journal and the pages of other journals identical to it since he passed! I envision many volumes filled for him (I wrote back then when I bought the first journal), or surely for as long as I live.

This is the first time I have ever described these journals that are Holy to me except in one book *In Corridors of Eternal Time*. I have even hesitated to do so now but have reached a peace about it in the hope that this might help others who are grieving and relate just how significant a cover can be.

And in addition to all these journals I have filled since his passing, I have written five books to help people all published by Blue Dolphin Publishing and this new one. But the writing was essential to my own soul. The books that I wrote that I have just mentioned were like keeping a journal also, and in a need to help others. I write and write. It is necessary for the soul. And I have a great desire to let others too know about this spiritual help. Journaling is needed for all aspects of life. Grieving is only one.

When you slow down and learn to experience wonder and awe, the mystery of it takes you deeper and deeper. These are moments to write about in our journals. Awe is spiritual. When we appreciate what we experience and even know we have to accept the pain, we are more aware and we live in the moment. We do not have to understand everything that fills us with awe and pain. That is the mystery of it. Write about it. Think upon it, and capture the essence of it all in your journal. It is like conversation and prayer. Write and write and write.

Amen

A poignant thought filled with truth I share with you now to ponder in relation to keeping a journal and in all aspects of life. I have known it since I was a child when the one who spoke it often reminded me in love of its significance.

Remember—there is only one you.

—Violet M, Gray (my very colorful Mother
whose names were two colors)

Rochester, beloved feline companion, confidant, counselor,
and ministering angel, finished his work here
after almost 16 years (minus one month) and passed on.
He was a motivator and enabler to me and
unselfishly gave of himself in deep love continually.
He was with me every day—all day while I wrote—
since he was eight weeks old and was my inspiration.
He was with me through every night.
Rochester was the Star of every book I wrote.
He was a most loving friend to Bob.
His sudden illness, diagnosed only Thursday, March 7th,
brought about his reluctant departure.
We were with him 'til he passed—and after.
He shall forever be with me in soul and spirit,
to help and inspire until we are together once more.

Rochester entered Heaven
March 8, 2002
5:07 PM

A Remembrance

"ROCHESTER"
T. PETERSON 7/03

Life-like 5x7 portrait of Rochester created by artist Tom Peterson, a gift from Tom and Sue Peterson from Colorado that arrived the very day that Rochester's book *In Corridors of Eternal Time* was finalized. It appears also in *Solace of Solitude, A Pilgrim on Life's Road, Cherishing* and *Silent Keepers*. This portrait has been drawn by a loving man I have never met and came to me in a handsome frame. How precious my friends have created such a gift for me. It indicates too the power of love and inspiration my Rochester causes to emanate to others. Tom and Sue have many beloved animal companions of their own and extend help to other animals in many ways. Rochester introduced us through Sue's reading of my *Journal of Love.*

Sweet Release

Robert A. Kolb Jr.

Piano

(1) When world-ly cares press in on me. — When dark de-pression and miser
(2) When app-re - hen - sion fills my mind. — When problems cause a deep mental
(3) When I for - get to dai - ly pray. — When I stray off of the straight narrow

y — sep-er - ate me from God's peace. — I turn to Jesus and find sweet re-lease.
bind. — When daily pressures won't cease. — I turn to Jesus and find sweet re-lease.
way. — When my life needs a new lease. — I turn to Jesus and find sweet re-lease.

CHORUS
Quiet peace then floods my soul. When I turn to Jesus and find sweet re - lease.

*J*ANICE KOLB, along with her husband Bob are the parents of six grown children and have nineteen grandchildren and two great grandchildren. Their life has revolved around raising a loving family with religious values. In addition to raising their family, Janice developed a letter writing and audio tape ministry that gives encouragement and spiritual support to those who need it all over the United States.

Other inspirational works published by Janice Kolb include:

Higher Ground
Compassion for all Creatures
Journal of Love
The Enchantment of Writing
Beneath the Stars and Trees,,,there is a place
Beside the Still Waters
Silent Violence
In Corridors of Eternal Time
Solace of Solitude
A Pilgrim on Life's Road
Cherishing
Silent Keepers
In a cooperative effort Janice wrote the book *Whispered Notes*,
with her husband Bob

***

Any correspondence to the author may be addressed to :

Janice Gray Kolb
P.O.Box 5
East Wakefield, NH 03830
jan@janicegraykolb.com

***

Visit her website at
www.janicegraykolb.com

227

Silent Keepers

Ellis and Rochester — Then and Forever

ISBN: 978-1-57733-227-5, 284 pp., 48 photos, 6 x 9, paper, $17.95

Jan Kolb recalls her father, whose strength and steadiness, love and wisdom were exactly the factors she needed in her life. She also honors Rochester, her beloved feline companion, who providing comfort and companionship when life seemed more than difficult. Both Ellis and Rochester were true "keepers"—that is, someone you want to keep and stay close to, no matter what happens.

Cherishing

Poetry for Pilgrims: Journeying On

ISBN: 978-1-57733-205-3, 368 pp., 76 photos, 6x9, paper, $19.95

This is a book not only of poems, but comments about the source of inspiration. Poems can make you laugh, cry, feel love, experience anger, and discover much about yourself. It's a different kind of a poetry book, and one you are sure to enjoy.

Beside the Still Waters

Creative Meditations from the Woods

ISBN: 978-1-57733-122-3, 276 pp., 11 illus., 6x9, paper$16.95

Jan's personal view of prayer suggests a variety of ways to be in constant contact with God. These meditations can transform your prayer life into a source of fulfillment, power and strength. Many of these prayers may be familiar; others may be new to you. Being open to all that you read, you may discover new pathways to God and loving consolation.

In Corridors of Eternal Time

A Passage Through Grief: A Journal

ISBN: 978-1-57733-135-3, 272 pp., 38 illus., 6x9, paper, $16.95

The book is a passage through grief, written in journal form. It explores dreams, visions, walking, memory loss, depression, examples of ways humans have grieved, journal writing, ways to help ourselves, and through it all, the passage through mourning a beloved companion.

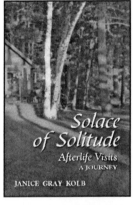

Solace of Solitude

Afterlife Visits: A Journey

ISBN: 978-1-57733-153-7, 300 pp., 6x9, paper, $17.95

This book was begun to find consolation after the sad events of 9/11. Then the death of Jan's beloved companion, her cat Rochester, exposed her to a new view of life and death. She describes what she experienced and realized as a result.

A Pilgrim on Life's Road

Guidance for the Traveller:
A Continuing Journey

ISBN: 978-1-57733-176-6, 184 pp., 6x9, paper, $15.95

A Pilgrim on Life's Road is the last of three by Jan Kolb to deal with grief—along with *In Corridors of Eternal Time* and *Solace of Solitude*. It completes the author's travels to the place where questions and aberrant thoughts have been dealt with. This does not mean that there is an end to grief, but grief has achieved a new dimension and now contains elements of resolution. The resolution of grief is not a single event, but a journey, which returns us not to what we were—for grief leaves an indelible mark—but to a place where growth can take place.